EDUCATION THROUGH ART IN AUSTRALIA

. . . because rhythm and harmony find their way
into the secret places of the soul, on which they mightily
fasten, imparting grace, and making the soul graceful
of him who is rightly educated . . .

—*The Republic* III . 402
Jowett's translation

AN AUSTRALIAN COUNTRY SCENE
Peter Edrupt (13), Northcote High School, Victoria

Education through Art in Australia

Edited by BERNARD SMITH

With an Introduction by HERBERT READ

MELBOURNE UNIVERSITY PRESS

First published 1958
Printed and bound in Australia by
Melbourne University Press, Carlton, N.3, Victoria
Registered in Australia for transmission by post as a book

London and New York: Cambridge University Press

Dedicated to
MAY MARSDEN and FRANCES DERHAM
teachers who, over many years, were the
courageous and indefatigable pioneers
of creative art education in
New South Wales and Victoria

Preface

This book will give everyone who is concerned with education in Australia a good deal to think about. It contains the most recent and the most progressive Australian thought concerning the place and the practice of art in education. Teachers of art, and all those preparing themselves for the profession will find it a most stimulating, readable, and thought-provoking guide to creative art education.

The book has arisen from the discussions of the UNESCO Seminar on the Role of the Visual Arts in Education which was held at the University Women's College, Carlton, Victoria, from 7 to 11 June 1954. The Seminar brought together from all over the country for the first time in its history, artists, teachers, inspectors, and administrators whose professional work brings them into daily contact with the problems of art education. The Seminar was, therefore, as truly representative of Australian thought on the subject as any seminar of its size could possibly have been. Consequently its conclusions were the fruits of years of thought and experience.

The Melbourne Seminar was sponsored by the Australian National Advisory Committee for UNESCO in the hope that it would follow up the fine work done at the UNESCO Seminar on the Teaching of Visual Arts held at Bristol, England, during the summer of 1951, which was attended by some forty people drawn from twenty different nations. The Bristol Seminar set out to examine the theory and practice of visual art education at different levels and in various types of educational institutions with reference to conditions prevailing in various countries, and to consider the ways in which the teaching and appreciation of the visual arts might enrich national cultural life and contribute to international understanding.

The Melbourne Seminar, broadly speaking, set itself similar terms of reference but, naturally, directed its attention more especially to the conditions and the problems of art education in Australia. Even so, it will be found that the contributors to this book, all experts in their own fields, have many refreshing and original observations to bring to the current international discussion concerning the place of the visual arts in the educational process.

A word about the contributors to this book. The introduction has been written by Sir Herbert Read. His own publications concerning art and education have been as widely discussed in Australia as elsewhere, and an Australian audience will appreciate his continued interest in educational reform here. The first chapter, 'Art and the Australian Community', is by Joseph Burke, *Herald* Professor of Fine Arts in the University of Melbourne. Since his appointment in 1947, when the Chair of Fine Arts (the only one of its kind in Australia) was established, Professor Burke has become known throughout the country for his services in the cause of art both within and beyond the University. The second chapter is written by Desiderius Orban, Chairman of the Australian UNESCO Advisory Committee for the Visual Arts 1953-5. Beginning his career as one of the pioneer artists of the modern school of Hungarian art, Orban is one of the best-known artists in Australia today and is also widely revered as a gifted and stimulating teacher.

The third chapter is by O. A. Oeser, Professor of Psychology in the University of Melbourne. The natural creativeness of children and its usually fatal contact with the stereotyped attitudes imposed by society is one of Professor Oeser's special interests and his essay should be brought to the notice of everyone in the country charged with the care of children. In the fourth chapter, his findings as a psychologist are borne out fully in the teaching practice of John Dabron, Supervisor of Art in the Education Department of New South Wales, and Chairman of the Australian UNESCO Advisory Committee for the Visual Arts, whose refreshing and imaginative approach has done so much to revitalize art education in New South Wales in recent years.

In chapter five Dr L. Hirschfeld Mack, himself an artist and a former pupil of Walter Gropius at the Bauhaus School, Dessau, Germany, tells how he teaches art to the boys of Geelong Grammar School. It is to be hoped that his creative and educative use of materials, an extension of Bauhaus principles, will help to bridge the gulf that divides creative art education from the uninspired, stereotyped teaching of craft that is still permitted in so many Australian schools.

Chapter six has been written by Sir Daryl Lindsay, formerly Director of the National Gallery of Victoria, to show how it became possible to bring the resources of a great gallery to the services of art education throughout Victoria; and in the following chapter, Gordon Thomson, the Assistant Director of the Gallery, grapples with the complicated problems concerned with the training of art teachers and the many unwarranted difficulties that they must still face if they continue to devote themselves throughout life to their profession.

In chapter eight Colin Badger, the Director of the Victorian Council of Adult Education, discusses the methods which have been used in Victoria since 1947 to stimulate a creative and intelligent interest in art in adult education. It would be heartening to see many of these methods applied more widely throughout Australia.

In chapter nine J. A. Campbell, Supervisor of Art in the Department of Education of Western Australia, discusses the question of 'Art and International Understanding' and tells of some of the ways in which the Bristol Seminar, which he attended as a representative from Australia, sought to use art in the cause of international understanding. And in chapter ten, Hal Missingham, Director of the National Gallery of New South Wales, considers the role that art can play in giving vitality to life in present-day society, so bound down with routine, gadgets, and second-hand emotions.

Chapter eleven is devoted to the new art syllabus for Victorian secondary schools which comes into existence in 1959. This syllabus is the result of a good deal of creative thinking by art educationists both in Victoria and abroad during the past ten years, and may be taken as one of the concrete results which have emerged from the opinions and attitudes to art education expressed in this book. Chapter twelve provides some interesting facts, submitted to the Melbourne Art Seminar of 1954, concerning the state of art education in three other Australian states: New South Wales, Queensland, and Western Australia. An appendix provides a list of the resolutions passed by the seminar, together with a list of the participants.

I am indebted to the members of the Australian UNESCO Committee for the Visual Arts for help and advice and especially to Mr H. K. Coughlan, Secretary of the Committee, Miss Florence J. Kendall, Acting Principal, Kindergarten Training College, Kew, Victoria, Miss Helen Wedd, Headmistress, Firbank, Sandringham, Victoria, and Miss R. E. Powell, Principal, Presbyterian Ladies' College, Burwood, Victoria, for their friendly co-operation in the provision of suitable photographs. Mr John Dabron kindly made available for reproduction a number of paintings from his excellent collection of children's paintings from New South Wales public schools.

Finally, it is, perhaps, not too late for me to thank Miss Myra Roper and her staff of the Women's College, University of Melbourne, for the courteous hospitality and generous assistance which, four years ago, did so much to make the seminar, from which this book has arisen, a pleasant and thoroughly worthwhile undertaking.

B. S.

University of Melbourne
        August 1958

Contents

Illustrations

xiv

Introduction

The Bristol Seminar of 1951, to which Dr Bernard Smith refers in his Preface, was organized on a modest scale, but thanks to UNESCO (and the enterprise of Mr Trevor Thomas, the UNESCO officer in charge) it was of wide international scope. What was unexpected, however, was the almost apocalyptic nature of the enthusiasm that developed during those few days, and that was carried to the four quarters of the globe when the delegates dispersed. This volume confirms the evidence that comes from Japan and Sweden, Germany and the United States, Brazil and Jugoslavia—in almost every country in the world there is now a realization that education through art (rather than art education) is a subject that transcends the narrow categories of vocational or specialist education.

The reasons for this are complex, and most of them are discussed by one or another of the contributors to this volume. But if I may use this opportunity to summarize a complex subject, I would say that though the need for a reform in the methods of art teaching as such have for long been apparent, and have indeed for long been recognized by all but a few die-hards of the academic tradition, the more basic implications of the movement are still not widely appreciated by the general public.

Education through art has a more than vocational or professional significance for two reasons. The first of these is psychological, and will be found clearly stated in Professor Oeser's contribution. The reason was stated clearly enough by Plato also, more than two thousand years ago. The development of an integrated personality, a peaceful and harmonious soul, depends on the capacity of the individual to establish an equilibrium between the inner world of instincts and desires and the outer world of intractable matter: on the ability to mould our environment into satisfying (and Plato would add, ennobling) patterns. Psychic equilibrium (or sanity) implies for man something more than a capacity for survival in the biological sense. Since we have evolved self-consciousness, we require, not merely animal satisfaction, but the mental condition which we call variously contentment, serenity or happiness. The creative activity, the capacity to mould our environment into satisfying patterns, is the most direct and positive way of achieving this mental condition.

Part of the outer world to which we have to adapt ourselves consists not only of things, but also of other people. We live in group-families, cities, nations. We need to communicate with these 'other people', and for that purpose we have developed various languages. To express our rational thoughts we have a system of signs, highly organized into word-systems and logical syntax. But a verbal language cannot communicate our irrational, or super-rational, moods, emotions, intuitions. For that purpose we have developed symbolic discourse, a language not of words, but of icons—'perceptible forms expressive of human feeling' (Susanne Langer). Art is a generic name for this symbolic language in all its modes. The function of art is to create and perfect the forms that constitute this symbolic language, with the intention of conveying to human sensibility a kind of knowledge that cannot be conveyed by any other means.

On the exercise of this creative activity depends the development of sensibility itself, and it is for this reason that art is so important in the intellectual and even in the productive (industrial) life of mankind. Fundamentally, the sciences depend on instruments sharpened by the arts.

It might be added that it is above all in a pioneer country, where there is no inherited background of symbolic images, no 'artistic heritage', that it is essential to cultivate the creative activities. A people cannot become a nation, in the cultural or historical sense, until the communal life is expressed in appropriate and enduring works of art.

Which brings me to the final and not the least important aspect of education through art. However harmonious in behaviour and serene in temperament, a man is not happy unless he can participate in group activities. Most activities of this kind are in the nature of games and play, which we should not deplore. Art itself is a kind of play, and indeed, as Plato again said, life itself is best regarded as a kind of play. Most play exhausts us physically (pleasantly so); but art is a kind of play that vitalizes us—above all, vitalizes the community. That is why, in the long perspective of history, the periods that stand out distinctively and elicit our deepest sympathy and admiration are those in which art has flourished.

I see no reason why, if it follows the wise principles set out in this book, Australia should not develop an art of this enduring kind.

HERBERT READ

I

Art and the Australian Community

JOSEPH BURKE

In Australia there is a gulf between the artist and his social environment. This gulf or separation is a feature of most industrialized societies, and I have no sensational new nostrum to propound. From William Morris to Sir Herbert Read there has been an increasingly informed diagnosis of the common disease, or rather group of diseases; and there has also been an increasing measure of agreement about certain remedies. The question is, therefore, not so much why things have gone wrong but how and where to concentrate the energies of a reform movement. The problem is particularly urgent in a young and expanding country, the greater part of which has been developed within the last hundred years.

Australia has, for a young country, been remarkably rich in artistic talent; for, by what may seem a paradox, it is frequently the offshoot of an older country and tradition which is most conservative. The story begins with a colonial phase, the most beautiful memorials of which are to be found in New South Wales and Tasmania; European vision is slowly adapted to the challenge of a new environment. There follows a rapid nineteenth-century expansion which reaches its climax in the late Victorian exuberance of the Boom Period. The mansions of Toorak are already in existence when Australian Impressionism, deriving simultaneously from the School of Barbizon and the contemporaries of Monet, is established by Streeton, Roberts, Conder and Frederick McCubbin, all of whom studied overseas. This tradition of overseas study has been of decisive importance; today there are few countries whose progressive painters are more closely linked with the School of Paris.

The vitality of present-day Australian art has been recognized by several distinguished visitors from abroad in recent years. Sir Kenneth

Clark, when he visited Australia in 1949, referred to 'a young and vital and adventurous school of painting'.[1] Dean Burchard, who came two years later, drew attention to the vigour of our *avant-garde* architects, notably Mr Roy Grounds;[2] and similar views have been expressed by other overseas authorities, including Walter Gropius and Sir Colin Anderson (Pl. 5, 6).

But the vitality of this achievement stands out against a forbidding background of public indifference and neglect. There is little official recognition of contemporary movements, apart from the enlightened policy of some of the state galleries, and still less from industry and commerce. What is the point, we may ask, of sending our best young painters and architects overseas, if what they learn precludes them from the chance of survival at home? And is not this critical situation further aggravated by progressive teachers, who secure the loyalties of young students even if they do not later travel overseas?

Standards of popular taste are almost uniformly debased. The artist who does not conform to these standards survives partly by the support of a small élite of private collectors, and partly by part-time employment as a teacher or commercial artist. He is thus a rebel against certain conditions of his environment, and amongst these must be included a system of art education, inherited from nineteenth-century England, and largely determining the attitude to art of a majority of the population.

When I first arrived in Australia I was struck by the remarkable influence of the Royal College of Art in South Kensington, as it was before the period of its first reform under Sir William Rothenstein. South Kensington had indeed trained inspectors and teachers whose influence in this country it would be hard to over-estimate. Children were still being taught in some schools to draw 'correctly', according to the laws of perspective, from models as uninteresting as they were simple; and to fill rectangular and circular shapes with floral motives, according to various repetitive formulae. The child is father of the man. The adult was formed under this system to admire unimaginative realism and stereotyped floral decoration, and somehow to associate these with art. Small wonder that today he dismisses some of the greatest achievements of contemporary art and the art of the past as so much mumbo-jumbo on the one hand, and barbaric crudity on the

[1] *The Idea of a Great Gallery*, Melbourne, 1949, p. 14.
[2] *Architectural Record*, August, 1952.

other! Or that he thinks of art, when he thinks of it at all, almost exclusively in terms of realistic easel-painting or applied decoration.

It is the first duty of the art teacher to combat these narrowing misconceptions implanted by a radically false method of teaching. Art is a whole environment. It embraces almost everything man-made in this environment, from industrial products to handicrafts; for what is there made by man in which the element of design does not play its part? Artistic values enter alike into the choice of cars, clothes, offices and their equipment, homes and their contents. D. H. Lawrence wrote that the factory could become the Parthenon of the future before the Bauhaus, or the General Motors Research Laboratory at Detroit by Saarinen, made his prophecy seem credible. The creative gift of the artist is not destined simply for the enjoyment of a handful of collectors, or to justify an occasional visit to an art gallery; it should be used to shape and inform the whole social environment of an age. So it was in primitive societies as much as in the greatest periods of western civilization, in Periclean Athens, medieval France and Renaissance Italy; so is it not, alas! today.

Although this gulf between the artist and his environment is not peculiar to Australia, it has, as I have mentioned, a special urgency in a young country. The first priority of the teacher is therefore the re-education of the community in the nature of art as a creative activity informing all aspects of human life. Today the citizen is scarcely aware that millions of pounds of the taxpayers' money are expended annually on artistic commissions: government buildings, offices, schools and ordnance factories. He would be still more surprised to learn that he himself, as the source of this expenditure, is a patron of the arts; as surprised, perhaps, as the character in Molière who discovered that he had unwittingly been speaking prose all his life.

The British Council (before its admirable activities in this country were so tragically cut down) did something to combat what might be described as the pictorial misconception, by sending out an exhibition of agricultural implements as works of art. Industrial design has recently, and in the same spirit, been included in the syllabus of Victorian schools with a wide range of examples including machinery and scientific instruments. One of the most costly errors of our time has been the hitherto prevailing and exclusive identification of art with the pictorial and decorative. Is it surprising therefore that the present age, with its ill-designed industrial environment, should be the ugliest in this history of civilization? If a factory by Saarinen, or a block of flats by Le Corbusier, can be seriously discussed in the textbooks of contemporary architecture, do not all factories, and all workers' dwellings become an artistic responsibility?

It is to governments, and to industry and commerce, that the artist today must look for his main opportunities. Since our country is expanding so rapidly, and such vast sums of money are to be spent on new buildings and their contents, the urgency of the situation can hardly be over-stressed. I should like to suggest two methods of approach to the problem. The first may be described as a five-year plan, and the second as a twenty-five-year plan.

The five-year plan concerns design in industry. A Society of Designers in Industry has been formed, the activities of which deserve high praise. It is a professional body, concerned primarily to raise professional standards, but it has also undertaken educational projects, including the preparation of film-strips for schools, and has conducted enlightened propaganda by exhibitions and publications. This body has been complemented by the Industrial Design Council of Australia, inaugurated under the chairmanship of Mr Essington Lewis at a special meeting held in Canberra in October 1957. The council is composed of leading representatives of industry, commerce, government and the civil service, as well as the designers themselves, and will be independent of government control.

At present Australian commerce and industry are highly protected, but in the long run our policy of protection can only be justified by its results. Who can doubt that if the present tariffs were removed there would be an overwhelming challenge to the locally manufactured product on the score of design alone?

I believe that the council has it in its power to effect very great changes in the aesthetic standard of our social environment within a period of five years. Furthermore, Australian industry would stand a better chance of export and of survival against the competition of more design-conscious nations, particularly the U.S.A. The talent is here in our young designers, as recent exhibitions have shown; it is only a question of harnessing it, and harnessing it quickly.

Fortunately the council has decided to make an immediate appeal to the public by a programme of awards and exhibitions. Through its membership it can reach at the highest level a large number of industrial and commercial organizations each with its own highly developed public relations machinery. It should not be too ambitious to hope that with a strong concerted drive the battle of principles and standards will be quickly won on the small but decisive front of enlightened leadership. At the same time the attack on the wider front of public opinion will be launched at many points, by information centres, industrial design wings in the art galleries, lectures and discussions under the sponsorship of responsible organizations. Every manufacturer who makes an article, and every consumer who buys one is a patron of art, generally without knowing it. If the council can drive this point home, half the campaign will be won.

The twenty-five-year plan concerns art education. Education is of all the professions the one most accustomed to long-term thinking. The teacher builds for the future, and often does not live to see the result of his life's work.

Since I have stressed those errors of the past which this country shares historically with Europe and the U.S.A., I should like to pay a tribute to that progressive movement of reform which has already achieved notable results in Australia. If I propose three main aims of the art teacher today, it is not because they are unfamiliar but because they must always be in the forefront of our thoughts.

The first I have already mentioned; it is to teach art as a creative activity. We as teachers know that the faculty of creation is the birthright of all children, although it is too often stultified by faulty methods in the classroom. Our watchword can be summed up in a single word: creation, creation, creation.

In the decisive areas of this country the battle of child art has already been won in the post-war period. There is immense room for improvement, but there are few primary schools left where children are taught to imitate rather than create. It is therefore the techniques of encouraging originality and inventiveness, rather than the basic objectives, which fall to be discussed.

The situation at the secondary school stage, however, is not so happy. Too many pupils show a falling-off in their creative powers between the ages of twelve and sixteen. Fortunately the success of some pioneering schools can already be indicated. Nevertheless, much remains to be done. In this connection I should like to draw special attention to the fifth chapter of this book by Dr Ludwig Hirschfeld Mack on the study of materials as a technique for encouraging creative activity. When Dr Hirschfeld Mack was an original member of the

Bauhaus, he conducted certain experiments in the art education of the young. These experiments have not, to my knowledge, been continued in any other country, and I believe them to be of international importance.

The second aim is to teach that all great art bears the hall-mark of truth to its own age.

The third aim has also been touched upon; it is to teach art as a whole environment. Art enriches and intensifies our consciousness of life, not just part of our life, but all of it.

Here again there is no particular difficulty with small children. Such peculiarly modern phenomena as fire-engines, aeroplanes and space-ships have votaries as enthusiastic and sometimes as exclusive as cowboys and Indians, pirates and even family relationships. But at the secondary school stage, for reasons of which we are not yet fully aware, the pupil becomes critically conscious of his environment and feels the opposite pull of an artistically debased social background. The wells of creation dry up, and he tends to imitate the most commonplace and spurious models. In too many cases he moves away from the life of the imagination, from symbolism and a natural instinct for shape and colour, to an inhibited representationalism. The appearance of the external world is, of course, as proper a subject for the artist as the inner life of the spirit; but the interpretation of the former is no less governed by the laws of the imagination. The teacher here should not combat these tendencies, but rather harness them to a sustained creative activity.

Above all, he should accept the new critical consciousness. Boys and girls between the ages of twelve and sixteen should be encouraged to talk and argue about their artistic environment. The act of creation, in other words, should go hand in hand with a no less creative discussion of the external world.

Some teachers have been singularly successful in liberating in the adolescent pupil powers of symbolic expression. It is precisely these teachers who have trained other pupils to interpret the external world with the greatest command of the medium and artistic sensibility.

In encouraging creative discussion of the environment the teacher has certain powerful instruments at his disposal. The first of these instruments is visual aids. Today film-strips and photographs of contemporary architecture and industrial design can be secured by schools for the cost of a few shillings. The Visual Aids Department of the University of Melbourne, in collaboration with the Fine Arts Department, the Society of Designers in Industry and a number of distinguished experts, including critics and artists, has prepared a number of these film-strips, covering not only contemporary art overseas but also in Australia, and has undertaken to provide a nation-wide service on a cost basis.

The second instrument is the loan services of the national galleries in each state. Splendid work has already been done in the circulation of drawings and paintings in country districts. Something further, however, needs to be done if taste in general is to be improved. A scheme for the circulation of 'boxes' to schools in all states is most desirable. The National Gallery of Victoria is planning, with the support of the Education Department and the help of the Victoria and Albert Museum, to inaugurate such a scheme in Victoria. Each box will contain contemporary textiles, glass, ceramics, tableware, photographic sets of contemporary architecture, industrial design and planning and, not least, a selection of books and periodicals. The teacher in a country school is sadly cut off from libraries and art bookshops, and one can hardly expect him to subscribe to the *Architectural Review, Domus* and similar periodicals which he needs to keep in touch with the artistic development of our age.

A third instrument is the examination syllabus itself. On the recommendation of Sir Herbert Read, the absurdity of examinations in creative art has already been abolished in Victoria. Art is not something to be turned on under examination conditions once a year between the hours of ten and one, or two and five. Candidates now submit a folio of their best work; for the first time they are actually treated as if they were artists. There is something to be said for totally abolishing examinations in art but under present competitive conditions this would mean crowding art out of the curriculum altogether. In a transitional period the syllabus can and should be used to allow both teacher and pupil the maximum of freedom. Moreover, the written paper, if it is based not simply on historical knowledge but on critical discussion, can at least ensure that the achievement of Henry Moore, Picasso, Gropius and Le Corbusier, as well as that of the contemporary artists of this country, is put before the young and intelligently debated by them.

Those of you who are artists may perhaps feel at this stage that in this discussion of the social background, the artist himself is the uninvited guest. In all humility I wish to say that the survival and freedom of the artist is the goal of my argument. The teacher cannot guarantee genius, but at least he can try to secure those conditions in which genius is not thwarted, but finds its fullest expression.

The power of the teacher in society is a very great one, and carries a no less high responsibility. Is it too much to hope that, with the new aims and methods, something like a revolution in the appreciation of art can be achieved within a generation? Such a revolution, releasing in our community the springs of a new creative activity, may not unreasonably be expected to close that gap between the artist and his social environment which is so distressing a feature of our time. When this gap is closed, the new age will at last have a fair chance of taking its rightful place beside the great periods of art history in the past.

2

Creativeness in Visual Art

DESIDERIUS ORBAN

When we look at the art of cavemen, of Australian aborigines, of illiterate peasants, and of children, we can only conclude that a creative urge is born within us and reveals itself at the dawn of our mental development. It is equally certain that this urge manifests itself in the visual arts before extending to other forms of human creativity.

There must be a definite psychological reason why we begin by creating visual images and why the creative urge for music, drama, poetry, literature, and even dancing remains latent for a time when pictorial activities are already in full swing.

But here I must point out a conflict between the urge to create and the desire to imitate. They are fighting constantly with each other because creativeness and imitation are contradictory. The history of art shows that whenever imitation gets the upper hand, oppressing creativeness, art becomes insignificant.

It is very difficult to discover what happens to the child's creative impulse in the second decade of its life. Most theories seek an explanation by stressing the sex problems of the adolescent. I do not believe that the proper answer lies there. On the contrary, I firmly believe that if there were no disturbing influences coming from *outside*, creativeness would solve the adolescent's confusing problems. Therefore we must investigate the wrong we do the child who has turned his back upon creative activity.

Here, as always, we are struggling with the conflict of creativeness and imitation. The child at the start is always creative. I know only too well that people will say that the clumsy way a child expresses itself (which I call creative) is due to the lack of skill needed for imitation. But the question is whether the child wants to imitate at all.

Children's art is symbolic, as is all creative art. The symbols based

9

on the experiences of the mature mind of the adult artist and the way he uses them are created on a much higher level than the self-expression of a child. But the question is whether the desire to imitate reality, which is usually forced on the child during its adolescent period, is a help or a hindrance to creative expression in adult life. Many world-famous artists have revealed that they had great difficulty in getting rid of the effects of their academic training. One might well ask why is an academic training a handicap? The answer is: the more we acquire the skill to imitate reality, which is the foundation of all academic training, the more is our creative imagination handi-capped—for creativeness and imitation are contradictory. Creation is a painful process. To imitate reality by means of an academic training is a routine job. How few people have the will-power to choose the painful process of creation once they acquire the routine skill to imitate. Usually by the time the student leaves the academy as a skilled painter, he has ceased to be an artist. Though he can be the most excellent craftsman, if he is not creative he is no longer an artist, because art *is* creativeness.

I come now to a point which is vitally important. Many embittered arguments could be eliminated if we would distinguish between painters and artists. To be a painter is to learn a trade like making boots or cabinets. To be an artist is to use one's creative imagination. Creative imagination is not as rare a gift as many people think. It is born with us. What is rare is the will-power to fight against the conventions, to push aside the endless derogatory exclamations of friends, relatives, neighbours, and critics of all kinds; and last but not least, it is rare to have the will-power to starve and to be deprived of appreciation because you don't want to follow the flock.

People are hostile to creativeness when they lose their own creative imagination during their up-bringing. Most people are not conscious of the fact that the most skilful imitation is still not art, because it pushes personality into the background. Art is and must be a personal experience in which the subject matter is only an excuse to create something which is symbolic in character.

I wish I could make clear what an unbridgeable gap there is between creative art and slavish imitation of reality; the satisfaction one gets from creating something out of one's own mind—whether it is based on reality or not—is different from the satisfaction of being so clever as to be able to paint a rose which looks like a rose in a gardener's catalogue. Even a portrait is a work of art only if it is creative. To make a hand-painted photograph is not a work of art no matter how similar it is to the sitter.

Skilfulness is not a yardstick for art; I mean skill acquired not by personal experience, but through tuition. Great artists of the past and the present show very different degrees of this kind of skill, but their greatness is not to be measured by it. Those who believe that the more skilful an artist is, the greater he is, have the greatest difficulty in understanding the reason for the greatness of artists like Giotto, El Greco, Van Gogh or Cézanne. Let me quote a few sentences from a book on Giotto. I wish only to show with what earnest expectation we may take such a book in our hand. Most people will read it with the strong conviction that the scholar who wrote it is an authority on Giotto's art.[1]

It was then that Giotto arose. This young painter, hardly thirty years old, suddenly produced entirely new ideas which his genius helped him to realize. His ideas were realism and expressive life, and at this point Modern Art, Italian Art, springs into being.

Realism—we must be clear on this point. Giotto longed for the truth, but he did not know how to observe. No easy task this, since it took Italian painting two centuries to learn it. On the other hand, we must grasp clearly that Giotto had not the necessary technical means at his command. He knew neither perspective nor anatomy nor chiaroscuro, nor the science of colour. His landscapes are diagrammatic, his architecture imaginary, inconsistent and out of proportion; like every good Italian painter, he rejoiced particularly in the human form, but he never succeeded in drawing it in its separate parts. The observation is incomplete and the execution empiric. Giotto's realism is general and primitive. However, such as it was, this realism, with its ignorances and its imperfections was powerful enough to bring about one of the most important artistic revolutions that has ever taken place.

Our critic is struggling all the time to convince the reader on the one hand what a great painter Giotto was and on the other what shortcomings he had. He cannot see that either Giotto was not a great painter or that the knowledge which Giotto lacked is not necessary to make a great painter.

Actually we are dealing with two kinds of skill: one is the painter's equipment, acquired through academic training; the other grows and develops with personal experience and never comes to an end. The skill of a painter usually reaches its peak when he leaves the academy,

[1] *The Great Painters—Giotto* (The Medici Society, London, 1931), pp. 3-4.

and reveals itself in endless repetition until he dies. The quality of his work starts to decline when he reaches the age of thirty or forty, by being constantly repeated. The creative artist, on the other hand, enlarges his experiences whenever he starts a new work. With every fresh attempt he tries to solve a new problem, without knowing what will be the end-result. His art develops, changes, modulates, until the last brush stroke of his last painting. It is a pulsing, living force and his skill grows equally with his maturing mind, but this skill is inseparable from his aim. It so happens that quite often a late work of a creative artist seems to be less skilful than an earlier one, if we separate means and aims. But this is just what we can't do. Means and aims are one and the same thing in creative art. I stress this strongly because it is a crucial point. The creative artist, whether he is five or fifty, has always at his command the necessary skill to express himself.

Children, as well as grown-up artists use self-created symbols. If a child draws a long arm with a lot of little things hanging from it, they symbolize fingers. If there are more than five that is his own concern as a creative individual. His symbols are more convincing and far more exciting than the dead reality of a painting which looks like a photograph.

Now a most conflicting process starts in the child's mind when grown-ups tell him that we have only four fingers and a thumb. From this point onwards the fight starts in the child's mind between creation and imitation. The great pleasure of creating symbols will be slowly replaced by the desire to imitate. Regrettably this desire can be fostered by showing children paintings of past periods when the skill of imitation was at a high level and creativeness at a low level. In such cases the adolescent makes an effort to try to be as skilful as these painters were, then, realizing the futility of it, turns away disappointed and gives up the whole thing.

These are the outside influences I have been talking about. The inborn conflict between dream and reality at the time of adolescence influences often badly enough the moulding of the character of the young. The desire of the adolescent to do something extraordinary could be turned marvellously into the channels of creativeness if parents and teachers would only encourage it. Instead of this, they show them things which are far beyond their own capacities, telling them: 'these are great works of art but you won't be able to do anything like this unless you put as much effort into it as the people did who made them'. So art becomes a burden instead of a thrilling pleasure for the growing personality and the most natural reaction is to push it aside and forget about it.

Unfortunately, it is not forgotten; it is only pushed into the subconscious mind where it starts its destructive work. It is a task of the psychologist to explain the mental process whereby creative children become hostile towards creativeness. And this is how our upbringing is responsible for misunderstanding and neglecting the vital importance of creativeness.

All this does not mean that if we leave the children alone they will all grow up creative artists. This is not even what we are aiming at. The task of the adult is to guide the child's mind into channels of creativeness.

Speaking of pictorial creativeness versus imitation of reality, the first step we must take is to distinguish between vision and mechanical sight. The child has a long way to go from the first time it perceives things until it can read without putting its finger on the line. During this period the eye is trained to see objects separated from each other; we are trained to have a sense of distances and to be able to focus the eye on the spot we are interested in. To be sure, without these implements we could not survive; we would touch the hot iron or would be run over by the approaching car. But this acquired skill, which is so vital in our everyday life, is useless for our creative activity. Looking at reality, the creative artist uses his perception which is just the opposite of mechanical sight. Instead of focusing his eye on any object, he has to learn how to see his subject matter as a unit. Instead of seeing one object at a time he has to see all objects at once. By doing this, he has a personal sensation of how the shape of one object influences the shape of another. In this way he perceives a relation of forms which the objective camera or our eye, trained by everyday experiences, cannot see. In this way, the experience of the artist is a personal one and his desire to make a picture, as I said before, has to solve a new problem whenever he sets out to paint.

I hope that all I have said is convincing enough to establish that creativeness should be the base of our education. Surely, when we speak of 'education through art', we do not mean that more bunches of flowers should be painted in a conventional manner. It means that if our whole education were based on creativeness, for which the best implement is creative art, the development of the character and later the philosophy of life of the adolescent, would be built on a solid foundation. The child would not then be put in a Procrustean bed, where, generally speaking, our educational system does put him. Different personalities would be moulded differently and the two main evils of our upbringing would be eliminated—fear of freedom and fear of responsibility.

I use the expressions freedom and responsibility in slightly different ways from those generally used. No doubt many people would strongly object to the accusation of being afraid of freedom and responsibility, but the freedom we are dealing with is the freedom not to be conventional, the freedom to break away from a routine life. It would not happen that on Monday morning at eight o'clock, the neighbour's wife would knock at the kitchen door asking whether madam is sick, because she can't see any washing on the line. Most people who do routine work all their lives, being on holidays, either do other routine work or become restless. What a godsend it would be for them if they were able to use the freedom of their imagination. But they can't, because they don't know how to. They are afraid of it. Most of their hobbies are based on set principles. Conservatism is fear of freedom. People are afraid to take a pencil in their hand, and draw something. Anything. If you urge them to do so, they answer 'I couldn't draw a matchbox'. If you assure them it doesn't need to be a picture of reality, you still can't persuade them to draw a single line.

Creativeness is a combination of freedom and responsibility.

The general manager of a business organization would laugh at you if you were to tell him that he is afraid of responsibility. But responsibility which is forced on us has nothing to do with creative responsibility. If people have the choice to do routine work or to create something which was never seen before, for which they and they alone are responsible, they will choose the routine work. Painters who paint conventional paintings do so because they are afraid of using their imagination freely. The closer you copy nature the less you are responsible for the result.

By imitating nature or other artists, you try to hide your personality. But whether you are a copyist or a creative artist your personality will be shown in your work for all those who can penetrate into it. A spectator of this kind is like a graphologist who sees your character behind your handwriting. The emptiness of mind of a non-creative

1 Qantas Building, Elizabeth Street, Sydney
Architects: Rudder, Littlemore and Rudder

What is there made by man in which the element of
design does not play its part? — Joseph Burke, *page* 3

2

We try to analyse materials . . . guided by certain laws of our present-day form of achievement — L. Hirschfeld Mack, *page* 34

3, 4

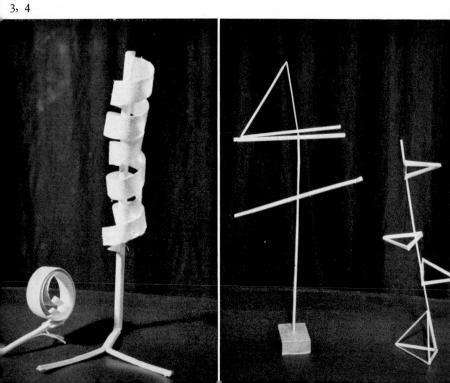

5

The vitality of present-day Australian art has been recognized by visitors from abroad
— Joseph Burke, *page* 1

6

7   *The day the snake nearly bit Ricki, while my sister and I were along the channel bank*

Pam Oakley, Infants' School, Griffith, New South Wales

I know only too well that people will say that the clumsy way a child expresses itself (which I call creative) is due to the lack of skill needed for imitation. But the question is whether the child wants to imitate at all — Desiderius Orban, *page* 9

The Bristol Report suggests that the general condition operating in many countries is a firm opposition by the older (and often controlling) teachers to the application of advanced methods and principles — *See page* 44 artist can be clearly seen in his work no matter how skilfully he tries to hide it.

All this must be taken into consideration when speaking of education. Creative thinking can be of value in every subject taught. If the child's mind is moulded through creative art, it will become a habit for him to use it. Instead of memorizing and accepting things he will investigate what is behind them.

Brought up in this way people would have an understanding of the changing ideas of every coming period. They would not live in the past but in the future. Getting used to taking responsibility in art, people would take responsibility in life. In short, if you accept creativeness as an expression of imagination in art, your outlook on life will change towards enjoyment of freedom and enjoyment of responsibility. Thus through the international language of art there could be established an understanding among peoples which is one of the great aims of UNESCO.

3

The Importance of Not Teaching how to Paint

Some Psychological Factors in the Graphic Productions of Children

O. A. OESER

In modern schools teaching emphasizes knowledge and skill: the dates of history, the facts of chemistry, the accurate manipulation of multiplication tables and test-tubes, the rules of syntax. Examination papers test knowledge and skill, but they cannot test personality as a whole nor feeling and imagination in particular. I have never met a school-teacher who would be prepared to give full marks to an essay, however brilliant and creative, which was untidily written, badly punctuated or spelled.

Drawing and painting have similarly been regarded as skills that can be taught, or more accurately, that should be taught in a certain way. It marked a great step forward in the liberation of the creative activities of children when they became free to paint what they liked in class and when, as in Victoria recently, the attempt to set examinations in 'creative activity' was abandoned. But there are still far too many schools in which art classes are concerned only with neatness, accuracy and 'representation' or 'nearness to reality'.

This is not the place to enter the age-old philosophical and aesthetic controversy as to whether pictures are 'reflections' or 're-creations' of reality, let alone to ask what reality is. These problems can be simplified by asking what and with whom a child is trying to communicate when he paints a picture. If he draws a map to show his playmate how to get to his house, or a diagram to show how his bicycle works, he is communicating common and universal facts or knowledge. If he paints a picture to show how he felt about his holiday at the sea, or how he feels about a ball game or his parents, he is communicating private facts. The criteria for these two kinds of activities are quite different: the first must reflect 'truth' in a mathematical or scientific and impersonal sense for everyone; the second must and needs be 'true' only to himself. The first kind of drawing ability can be taught, and punishment for inaccuracy may help (if one believes that punishment e.g. disapproval, ridicule, is an indispensable tool for teachers). The second kind of drawing ability can only be encouraged—not taught—and punishment simply suppresses or murders it.

However, it is not only the teacher who suppresses the capacity of a child to express his own personal vision of people, places and events. He is aided and abetted by society, which creates social conventions or stereotypes about art and beauty; what a picture should look like.[1] He is himself a representative of adult society, charged with transmitting to the new generations the knowledge, skills and beliefs of the old. If a teacher departs too far from expectations, he is likely to get into trouble whether he is teaching history, science, literature or art.

The problem of the art teacher, then, has *four* aspects: to know enough about the developmental stages through which the emotions as well as the knowledge and skills of a child pass in order that the teacher may neither unduly force ahead nor retard and frustrate the developmental process; to understand (but not necessarily to approve) the aesthetic conventions and stereotypes of the society in which the teacher himself grew up; to communicate or transmit skills of draftsmanship and painting; and to have sufficient tolerance to be able to keep in the background his own predilections of the beautiful. None of these four aspects can be dealt with adequately here. But it may be worthwhile to examine some aspects of each and their interrelations.

It is instructive to carry out a simple investigation by asking children of different ages to make drawings or paintings with the titles 'headache', 'sad', 'angry man', 'tired mother'. One then readily sees that the pictures begin (at the age of five, say) by being quite free of stereotyped representation. Feelings are displayed through size and colour in an as yet quite uninhibited and dramatic fashion. For instance, a five-year-old made a small round sweep of purplish colour for a face, a small mouth and a dark broad streak on top of the head to symbolize 'sad'. 'Happy', by contrast, was a large circle covering

[1] See Helga Eeng, *The Psychology of Children's Drawings* (Kegan Paul, London, 1931).

almost the whole paper, vividly coloured, having a large mouth with bright locks running riot all over the head and sides. The contrast between the smallness of 'sad' (Pl. 8) and the generous size of 'happy' (Pl. 9) was as impressive as the difference in colour.

But from about the age of eight onwards, the pictures of happy, sad, angry or tired people differed only in small and often irrelevant details. The states of mind were often expressed by 'balloons' issuing from the mouth—'Hurray!', 'I hate you', or by bared teeth and deep vertical lines on the forehead for rage and deep horizontal lines or closed eyes for fatigue. Colour was hardly used to express emotion, except by one boy who drew in red crayon a clumsy outline of a man holding a cudgel.

At later ages, those who had achieved some mastery of draftsmanship expressed feelings occasionally by making a picture-story, but these were still highly conventional stereotypes. It seems that the power to express an *experience* had been inhibited somewhere about the age of six.

This contrast between the immediacy of registering a feeling in paint and the mere surface perception of lines and shapes was vividly illustrated in the series 'tired mother'. A child aged five drew an outline of half a body, the lower part of the paper being filled with heavy blue colour, as though the mother were being literally pulled downwards out of the picture to the ground. The children of ten to thirteen in the same school drew conventional women sitting on chairs or leaning on a broom, in a flat, 'uninspired' way. When the five-year-old's 'tired mother' (Pl. 11) was compared with Topolski's sketch 'The Warden' (Pl 10), the relation between the power of a great artist and that of a small child was obvious. Both illustrated the heaviness of fatigue by dark masses at the bottom, by enlarging those parts which one's experience told one were the 'carriers' of fatigue—Topolski's drawing, for instance, shows enormous boots and long heavy drooping hands, and even the cigarette in the corner of the warden's mouth droops downwards.

The child of five and the mature artist both have this power of conveying feelings, the majority of children have lost it. What has happened?

We do not yet know enough in detail about the way in which the impulse to communicate an intense personal vision is destroyed and even less about why it is maintained in some people. But we can

8 *Sad* Sonia (5)

9 *Happy* Diana (5)

12 *Miss Suzannah Gale*
Sir Joshua Reynolds
(National Gallery of Victoria)

13 *Miss Suzannah Gale*
Kerry Haberman (12), Firbank,
Church of England Girls' Grammar
School, Sandringham, Victoria

It is an excellent thing for children
to be brought to galleries and for
them to get the habit young of
going to galleries, so that they will
grow up in contact with the first-
rate — Sir Daryl Lindsay, *page* 42

We should see to it that in art
appreciation . . . the child is introduced to adult culture — Gordon
Thomson, *page* 43

14 *The Meat Delivery*
Donald Carvosso (13), Nailsworth Boys Technical High School,
South Australia

A classroom which adjusts the child to accept the creations
of his fellows—creations with fine or startling degrees of
difference—as all part of normal experience, is establishing
ability in comparative criticism and tolerance — John
Dabron, *page 25*

make some guesses. Loewenfeld[2] has shown that the young child and the expressionist painter have certain elements in common: both exaggerate those parts of a picture which *to them* seem important. The arm stretched out to reach a high apple is exaggerated; the hand which grasps a heavy weight is made large and thick; a statue modelled by a blind child and called 'Longing for Sight' has greatly enlarged hands and elongated arms while the rest of the body is quite puny. This, indeed, is how one's bodily proportions are experienced when one tries the experiment of closing one's eyes and stretching hands and arms upwards. They *feel* 'larger than life'. Similarly many feel small if they are alone in a large crowd in a strange city. Loewenfeld also showed that this 'haptic' way of drawing is retained by some, whereas others seem naturally to become 'visualizers' who draw and paint in proportions as they appear to the eye.

It is clear that all children progress from what, with Ehrenzweig,[3] might be called 'form-free unconscious perception' to 'surface-bound (or Gestalt) visual and tactile perception'. That some retain their 'queer' expressionistic angularity and concentration on subjective body sensations and feelings is not, as Loewenfeld assumes, because there are 'natural types'—visualizers and haptics—but means that normal development has been arrested. Why this happens in a given individual is a matter for psychoanalytic investigation and theory, and cannot be pursued here.

The general progression is not unlike that of play, which at first is symbolic, and later becomes more and more reality bound: at first a piece of wood may stand for a dog, a knife, a car; later either real objects or representational copies are used in games. In language development one also finds the same progression, from preoccupation with self to concentration on reality. One of the bitter lessons everyone has to learn is that words are not always magic formulae, and that a stone over which one stumbles is unmoved by punishments or commands, that real companions do not appear and do one's bidding as do the imaginary companions so many young children invent, and that to draw a circle round 'angry dog' is not in reality an act of power. Deep within us, of course, this magical outlook remains. Primitive peoples kill their enemies by sticking pins into a doll,

2 Viktor Loewenfeld, *The Nature of Creative Activity* (Kegan Paul, London, 1939).
3 Anton Ehrenzweig, *The Psycho-Analysis of Artistic Vision and Hearing* (Routledge & Kegan Paul, London, 1953).

primitive medicine men don masks to frighten illness away, or to lure the sick spirit into the mask as into a mirror of its own distorted existence.

Colour is the only medium that remains absolutely free. It can be used both to exhibit emotions and to blot them out. For instance, a little girl painted an 'angry man' in violent reds. Her picture was so expressive that it frightened her. So she took a large brush and overlaid her work with rapid strokes the effect of which was to form a black grille behind which the fearful object was safely imprisoned. But even the use of colour has been stereotyped by our society: the milk and roses of the chocolate-box woman, the square jaw and bronzed look of the he-man; trees are green and water blue; the innocent are blond and blue-eyed; the criminal is dark and squints.

That conventionalization is easily learnt by the child is not surprising. When the child begins to grow up, begins to master his contacts and conflicts with reality, he learns language. Words are designed for maximum uniformity of communication, so that for the ambiguity of feeling a vocabulary hardly exists. Words are also used to symbolize and express the values of one's own society: for an Australian, a 'white man' is potentially good, a 'black man' potentially bad or dangerous. In China, Europeans are thought of as being permanently angry or violent, because slant eyes are 'good' and are rounded only in anger. This process of stereotyping has become vastly accelerated through the invention of printing. Matisse in an essay on *The Nature of Creative Activity* has said that 'the cinema, posters and magazines present us every day with a flood of ready-made images which are to the eye what prejudices are to the mind'.[4] Moreover, poster and magazine pictures are themselves the final stereotyped caricature of the 'representationalist' theory of art, which has dominated our Western society for so long.

Before we turn to the educational implications of what has been said so far, let us consider a most illuminating statement in the same article by Matisse, himself a great artist:

The effort needed to see things without distortion takes something very like courage; and this courage is essential to the artist, who has to look at everything as though he saw it for the first time; he has to look at life as he did when he was a child and, if he loses that faculty, he cannot express himself in an original, that is, a personal way.[5]

4 *Education and Art*, ed. by Edwin Ziegfeld (UNESCO, Paris, 1954), p. 21.
5 Ziegfeld, op. cit., p. 21.

No one can be taught to reproduce what he has not seen. But seeing itself cannot be taught: it can only be encouraged by providing both the materials for experience and the social climate or occasions on which the child himself becomes imbued with the desire to explore visual, tactual movement and other sensory activities. Up to the age of about eight it therefore seems of vital importance not to instruct but to provide the occasions on which a child can and will want to communicate his experiences by means of painting. The means and forms he chooses will often seem surprising, even bizarre. Nevertheless the teacher should reinforce the effort by praise and should not insist on correcting let alone condemning.

It is necessary to bear in mind that any new activity or skill calls out the child's need to practise that function. Not until a new function has been practised over and over again *for the sheer pleasure of functioning* does the child proceed to regard its products as an end, as a 'job' or 'creation'. When he reaches that stage, he will be more concerned with the external effects of his activities, of their capacity to communicate impersonal facts. He will want to fit in with the accepted norms of his social groups. He will then begin to demand instruction in how to draw, say, someone sitting on a chair, or a distant perspective, how to make clear visually that this is a winter and not a summer sky.[6]

How this process of combining experience with the demands of reality begins is well illustrated by what Loewenfeld calls 'folding over'.[7] In a landscape containing a pond and a railway line these are drawn in plan whereas trees, ducks and railway carriages are drawn in elevation. This happens not so much because the young artist does not know how to draw ponds and rails in perspective, but because he wants to draw attention to those things which he feels are important to him. What is important is either exaggerated or drawn in its most characteristic (and therefore satisfying or impressive) appearance. The artist, then, is communicating both knowledge and feeling; and when the teacher emphasizes correct drawing he is likely to weaken seriously the impulse to paint. If, instead, he observes and asks tactful questions, he is likely to learn much about the child which may be of great help to him in his future guidance of the child. This is, of course, standard

[6] Detailed discussions of these stages of development can be found in Charlotte Bühler, *From Birth to Maturity* (Kegan Paul, London, 1935), chs. 5 and 6 especially.
[7] Op. cit., pp. 26, 43, 66.

practice in child guidance clinics, in which the paintings of disturbed children tell one far more, and more immediately, than the child can say in words.[8] While the child is painting 'this is how I feel about a walk in the country', he is schooling himself in seeing, in observing what things look like when he is in a certain mood and what they 'really' look like.

In some schools children are allowed to produce group pictures. An obvious occasion for such activities is scene painting for a play, but the activity need not have a practical aim. This practice seems well worth encouraging. When several children co-operatively make a large painting one finds that a tremendous amount of discussion develops. This is often much more vigorous, sustained and to the point than is discussion with the teacher, because it takes place among equals, and is uninhibited by adult norms and conventions. The activity is a better training ground both for 'seeing afresh with the eyes of a child' and for mastering some of the technical communication problems. The teacher who is acquainted with the theory and practice of the dynamics of small groups will, of course, be able to use such exercise to even greater effect.[9]

These discussions have implicitly been concerned with the problem of 'genuineness', 'correctness' and 'representationalism' in painting. The point of view put forward here is that of Piaget: 'Beauty, like truth, is of value only when re-created by those who discover it.'[10] The emphasis is on discovery, not on demonstration, on truth from the person's point of view, not on generalized, abstract, impersonal or logical truth.

It is easy to train the child to be anxiously concerned with not being found wanting in skill by his society. Indeed, Oeser and Emery[11] have shown that from the child's point of view school is a predominantly coercive institution, in which the learning of stereotypes is encouraged and the expression of a personal vision and of personal feelings discouraged.

At the beginning it was said that the ability to paint according

[8] Excellent case histories and colour reproductions can be found in R. H. Alschuler & L. W. Hattwick, *Painting and Personality* (University of Chicago Press, 1948).

[9] Why and how to use small groups in the classroom is set out in O. A. Oeser, *Teacher, Pupil and Task* (Tavistock Publications, London, 1955).

[10] 'Art Education and Child Psychology', in *Education and Art*, ed. by E. Ziegfeld, p. 23.

[11] O. A. Oeser and F. E. Emery, *Social Structure and Personality in a Rural Community* (Kegan Paul, London, 1954).

to one's own 'truth' is suppressed or killed very early by unimaginative adults no less than by the demands of society and of external reality. The painter Mark Tobey once showed that it can be revived in all, and made to grow into genuine talent in some. At Dartington Hall, a lovely estate in Devon on which a large-scale experiment in rural living has been in progress since 1925, he took a group of adults—estate workers, carpenters, gardeners, teachers, musicians—and encouraged them to express on paper ideas associated with feelings. It was remarkable to see how one adult after another first demonstrated the age at which his graphic impulse had been suppressed; how under Tobey's benign and permissive stimulation he began to experiment, to recapitulate earlier stages of drawing and to progress through later ones, and how finally—in a period as short as six months—some became good artists, able to design interesting pictures, and once again deeply concerned with techniques but at an immeasurably higher level.

The purpose of this paper has been to emphasize the importance of not teaching how to paint until the pupil feels the need to know, and then only if his need is not merely for conventional conformity. The Mark Tobey experiment showed that there is latent in most adults a real ability to paint. And why should this be surprising? All adults are capable of communicating ideas and experience through language; and the feat of learning a language is one of incredible complexity and difficulty. Why, then, should they apparently be incapable of communicating by the use of lines and colours? What would be the repercussions on art and design if a few generations of schoolchildren were allowed to see, to feel, and to paint as they saw and felt until with the due onset of maturity they determined to master the intricacies of graphic representation as diligently as they determine to master the many other technical skills through which society persists and grows?

4

Art Education and the Child

JOHN DABRON

To my mind, the principles which guide art education are: education at the emotional level, art as a means of expression, freedom in creative activity, and art as a means of communication and understanding. The most important words in these points are 'creative activity' and we should be very clear as to our meaning or interpretation of 'creative'. Let me enlarge on these points.

First, education on the emotional level. Emotion means the moving of the feelings. Education on the emotional level means engaging in practices which move the feelings, develop rich resources of feeling and thereby endow the child with a rich and ready response to the environment of things, people and thoughts. This brings about a better self and thus a better group member. Through wide experience of emotions will come a clearer understanding of them, which can then be better directed into channels more fluently creative and positive and, above all, non-destructive.

Second, art as a means of expression. Expression to me means bringing into being; transposing or transferring or translating one set of ideas, feelings, thoughts, into a medium which may communicate to others or back again to self. It is a communion with self that is of greatest importance, though the experience satisfies a social need when it communicates successfully with others. Satisfactory expression helps bring about a condition of personal ease. I don't necessarily mean self satisfaction, but a situation of internal betterment, not necessarily well being, which rather aids adjustment to environment, its people and problems.

Third, art as a means of communication and understanding. Speaking, singing, moving, acting, dancing, all are means of communication. So too are painting and drawing and modelling. Thoughts and feelings are pressed into a medium which conveys them in a satisfactory way, and the visual arts have their own unique appeal where words and sound and movement may be far less clear. The visual arts traverse both time and the world. They are direct communication where music and to a degree the other art forms have to be re-created or interpreted or reproduced. Visual art strikes direct from the creator to the beholder. It is the only direct form of communication that we have with the past.

A classroom which adjusts the child to accept the creations of his fellows—creations with fine or startling degrees of difference—as all part of a normal experience, is establishing ability in comparative criticism and tolerance. We live when world understanding is clearly important, even essential, and creative art is one of the ways of bringing about international goodwill and sympathy.

It is odd and interesting to reflect what thoughts rush to one's mind when one hears the word 'personality'. I immediately think of several things at once—the diaphragm, breathing, the spine; I am conscious of the mould and movement of the body, the voice and the glance, and indefinable energies, words and deeds, indeed of a whole sum of physical, mental and emotional components that makes the person a creation. In subtle and unique distinctions, differences, and characteristics, the personality is made and has individuality of mind, body and feeling.

Now art is unique in bringing out the individual quality of our minds and our emotions. In music as it is now taught I am afraid we are the slaves of the ordinary major and minor scales and the four-bar phrase. In speech we adhere to the conventions of our day, and in writing we have to be clear in conveying our meaning. But with art we are in a free world; we need not be clear, we may draw in any conceivable way at all. We may communicate any mood we find ourselves in, or we may tell of appearance, knowledge or feelings. While art is not just a game without any rules, it offers the greatest possible freedom so that those of all ages, mentalities and physiques may achieve success in expression and the needs of the individual be met. And in this connection we must remember that a personality which gains a strength in one of its facets will gain in others too.

Now, while giving lip service to these principles, a large proportion of teachers and authorities do not put them into full effect because they have not thrown aside incrustations of past techniques and prejudices. In a practical classroom, for instance, many children are not creative under the following circumstances:

1. When they paint in an inhibited, slow, frightened way.
2. When they paint in such a way that they solve no problem, surmount no difficulties.
3. When they go through exercises with minds on techniques instead of hearts alive with excitement.
4. When they try to emphasize the correct visual appearance of things.

Let me take these points in order.

Inhibited work. Why do children paint in an inhibited, slow, frightened way? Because they have a preconceived notion of the way they should paint (should I say the kind of pictures they should produce?), the result of early conditioning by the most harmful illustrations in infants' school books, especially in reading, fill-in, and cut-out books. But this is only part of the difficulty. Children are surrounded by pictures everywhere from the earliest age and are influenced by all forms of illustration, particularly commercial and strip pictures. When young they do not perceive the nature of the mould, but must advance through the several stages of their development unarmed and innocent against overwhelming, destructive, non-creative, bad art. Being accommodating creatures wanting to please their teachers, their parents and their fellows, they try to fit into the mould.

It is very interesting to note, however, that the dull ones keep on struggling to create after the bright ones give up. Those bright ones who have talent for visual representation prostitute it gracefully. They imitate, they do not create. The assertion that dull children are better at creative art than clever ones is nonsense. But the clever ones are also more able to fit into conventions of insincerity. Those who are clever enough to see that they can never succeed in the popular accepted visual representation or commercial style, give up. They won't even try to do something; they know too well they can't. They have not had the creative aspect of art stressed. They have never seen even reproductions of great art. The world of great art is closed to them. Children naturally prefer good painting to bad, but they reject their impulse to approve of it because of their home and school influences. Their parents and teachers would never single out a Braque, say, for notice and favourable comment, when everyone everywhere, the mass, approves or accepts inferior material (I avoid the word art).

I do not say there is a ready cure for all this, but there are at least two possible counter measures. First, see that the children have the opportunity of studying numerous—I mean hundreds—of examples of good art. Let them discover and let the teacher emphasize that any artist who is remembered contributed something to life that was personal. Second, make the children speed up, don't let them be slow. Frighten them out of their fright—into creativeness—and embolden them; praise creativeness, condemn imitation.

Children are not creative when they solve no problem, surmount no difficulty. I must explain that children are, of course, always at liberty to paint in a relaxed way, but then problems may be solved and difficulties surmounted in a relaxed way too. Problems may not even be apparent. The problems may arise during the work. Any move with line, colour, and tone demands complementary moves, juxtapositions and arrangements, and this in art is an ever-present problem. The problem, however, may arise from expression and interpretation of the subject. Is the expression adequate? Has the child given of his best feelings and thoughts or knowledge?

But the essence of the matter is this—that imitation denies creation and the child may soon imitate himself. Young ones of course appear to some to imitate themselves, but I believe that is rather re-creation and time brings the change. I refer to the later primary grades, where children are apt to churn out the same thing. The art lesson becomes routine, a stereotype develops. The solution is simple. Give the children new subjects and a change of medium. Agree to have an aim and solve the aim. Their degree of success is measured by reference to the aim and a variety of aims helps to avoid the stereotype.

The emphasis on technique. I regard art for young children primarily as an emotional experience. Age will bring the discipline of the intellect. Technique means ability in manipulation, the mechanics or method of performance. Some people regard so-called correct drawing, correct perspective, correct proportion, all leading us to correct visual appearances, as technique. But whatever we mean by technique we must remember that there are countless hundreds of techniques for each child, not one technique for all children. In manipulation there is always the chance of discovering new methods, and movement itself can engender emotion. The earliest manipulations of the very

young child range from a touch of the utmost tenderness to movements of amazing vigour and fluency, almost aggressive. The teacher
has to recapture this submerged energy, this lost sensitivity. With
this in view, the only technique that one should bother with is one
that involves movement, and a wide range of movement too, from
slow to fast; and of varying character and quality from the impulsive
to the considered, from the calm to the agitated. As for the correct
way to use a brush—different ways give different effects. Which effect
satisfies the need? What do you want, this or that? Which of course
is all very easy and the problem of technique vanishes.

Visual appearance. To be preoccupied with a statement of correct
visual appearances in art is not to create, it is to imitate. To the
artist of this and other centuries the rectangle, or other space, that
frames a picture is a world—a new world—to be filled entirely as
he wishes. It is not necessary to present to other men the same familiar
vision they can see for themselves. The artist in relation to the subject
is privileged to comment upon or to emphasize some aspect, or describe
in a personal way, or express his reaction, or to escape. A work of art
can be measured by the degree of success achieved in organizing the
elements of the design so that this world becomes a creation, a universe,
a cosmos, an entity. Visual appearances may be shown, yes, but in
such a way as to present the rhythm, the balance and the emphasis
in the newly created world of line, colour, and tone. The way this
is done depends on the personality of the artist.

I would like at this point to discuss guidance. The art lesson should
be regarded by the teacher and pupils as a convention—a coming
together (of up to forty pupils per teacher) for the purpose of making
an agreement, and the agreement is that an aim should be put forward,
discussed and the lesson carried out with the aim in view. This is
so that the group will achieve something as a whole. The aims can
be to say something about self, home, school, family; or to work
fluently, fill spaces well or to demonstrate harmony or contrast of
any of the art elements or to emphasize some principle. Each of
these aims presents its own problem and each may be solved in a
unique personal way, so that although the members of the group each
have the same aim, the execution is an entirely personal matter. By
varying the aim the group covers a wide range of experience and as
a result becomes more informed, more educated. Children are given
the means to evaluate their own work and other work too.

To illustrate: if I ask children to draw three dignified old ladies yet at the same time to show harmony of colour, the children are sure to hit upon the feeling of dignity in perpendicularity and to use this as a dominant feature of their design. The harmony of colour limits the child to a degree, but only to a degree, to establish a dominant key as it were. This is our convention, but within these small limits endless variety can be achieved. The work is entirely personal, with this achieved for education—the child can discuss and understand the quality and the effect of perpendicularity and harmony.

In this kind of lesson something has been learned; an intellectual satisfaction is added to the emotional satisfaction. The experience in this kind of lesson helps to develop awareness.

Guidance must always be of the kind that inspires the child to a higher standard, but never should the standard be so high that it discourages him. The adolescent is rampant with creative energy. His humour, his mischief, his sport are expressions of this. No longer is he naïve, he is becoming a man. I think the people who say that he has lost his creativeness in art, admit or infer their own inability to assess creative quality apart from child symbols; or they admit their failure to instil principles of creative art, to assist the child to conquer, assimilate, or exploit the influence of his environment. Teachers, in giving in to the child's wishes, are not helping him to overcome the difficulties of his environment. They fail in their duty to the child.

I am prepared to admit less need for guidance of a specific kind on such occasions as when the uninhibited child grows up and when his environment does not degrade his taste. In the meantime such tactics are necessary as will make him positively conscious of his potentialities as an artist in life. He will not be an artist professionally. But with a conviction of the importance of creative art, and with ability to organize the art elements in an agreeable way he will bring to his living a relaxed quality—adjustment, understanding, critical ability and a sense of order. And while it is accepted that youth is of course subject to the influence of its elders, and desires by nature to imitate them, their inspiration and leadership should come from great art of all time, especially art of their own time, of which they cannot see too much. Therefore their attention should be directed as they grow up to the art stream of the day for debate, discussion, and resolution. Participation in all possible art activities will make for a rounded personality in the adult.

The teacher of the child has the responsibility of guidance, and the nature of this guidance will decide in a large measure on the creativeness or otherwise of the child's work. Guidance should be given in such a way that the child restores and develops native abilities such as:

1. Fluency in movement and ideas
2. Awareness
3. Fantasy.

Fluency. I have mentioned fluency in movement and fluency in ideas. To the question when does the child cease to be completely creative I would say perhaps it is the day after the child has been told by the teacher that he is drawing a messy line or that he is wrong when he puts in four fingers instead of five. Immediately he has to stop to think what the teacher wants. His unity of purpose, his life, his personality, is split. If this process is continued his personality suffers considerably and if he is not able to satisfy the requirements of adults his output becomes crippled; in many cases it becomes negative.

A teacher should be sensitive to the closing up or shrinking of expressions and immediately he should examine the whole process of his classroom practice. Conflict with adults is usually the reason. Lack of ability or lack of brains, on the part of the child at least, is not responsible for retarded creative output.

Awareness. This means conscious, informed, or sensitive awareness of people—their ideas and feelings, and of things and their qualities. According to the individual there may be emphasis on visual awareness, or touch, or emotional awareness. I can only emphasize that development of this quality in the individual will provide a better member of society in later life.

Fantasy. This is wonderful for relaxation, but it is much more than that. By taking the real world and creating new juxtapositions according to whim or impulse, we demonstrate our ability in creating new relationships, new formulae. The great discoverers and scientists, to mention only Archimedes and Edison, must have possessed the gift of fantasy. Edison I know was a backward dreamer at school. I am not alone when I say that the world owes a lot to the artist, the artist in all walks of life, the dreamer. I think that whoever wrote the popular song 'Wake up and Dream' had something.

The teacher is further responsible for the child's feeling or understanding, through use and familiarity, the principles which help to establish a work of art. If guidance is to be effective it will be found that a set subject with an aim is necessary for progress, mainly because exchange of ideas in a group working on one theme in different ways can then be made, with emphasis on freedom of interpretation and sympathetic regard for other points of view. The child should be allowed the privileges that are enjoyed by contemporary artists. These are to paint a subject with emphasis on seeing, feeling, or knowing according to natural inclination and to experiment with media in an inventive way.

The artist creates an order out of the multitude of stimuli in our universe, and children, in their way too, can put together an agreeable arrangement of art elements. The practice of this from an early age will assure better art and living in adult life.

5

Creative Activity and the Study of Materials

L. HIRSCHFELD MACK

We introduced the study of materials in our preliminary course in the Bauhaus, a school in Germany for artists and architects, about thirty years ago. So the study of materials is certainly not new. This work was completely interrupted by Nazism but it has been continued in America by Joseph Albers who introduced it in his teaching of students and adults. It has not been introduced in schools with children in America, as Professor Gropius told me when he was in Corio.

If you observe children playing by themselves or in groups, you will find they are enthusiastic, concentrating intensely and so much united that they seem to be almost in the same psychological state as the artist, concentrated on one objective of creativeness, from which expression and serenity spring. It is most important that teachers endeavouring to understand children fully should observe their self-guided play activities outside the schoolroom.

If the school succeeds in transferring these qualities of enthusiasm, serenity and concentration, and of satisfying true curiosity and adventure, teaching will become a great satisfaction to both the children and the teachers, because they will learn from each other continually.

Work with materials, based on undisturbed play, should start in the kindergarten and continue up to the age of eleven to twelve years. Playing is the most natural and purest expression of the child's creative ability. That is why we start with playing only. But we start with playing also with older children and even with adults. Grown-up people like to play just as much. Many great inventions have been made accidentally—just by playing with materials, or through curiosity, for instance, trying to find the cause of a fault. In such a way Dr Röntgen discovered X-rays.

A child would certainly not play with a pointed pencil, a spiral sketch-book and an indiarubber, but he would play with sand, clay, earth, grass—anything within reach of his hands—with stones, sticks, straw, boxes, tins, cotton reels, with string, pins, needles and nails, with buttons, match-boxes and woodshavings, etc. Why not take these materials into the classroom? It is up to us to preserve the child's devotion and enthusiasm for his play and lead this play gradually to sincere work. Children often start by laying materials flat on paper or cardboard, sticking or pasting the materials on, adding colours afterwards. They do it individually or in groups—on tables, benches, or the floor, building houses, towers, aeroplanes, carts, engines, figures and animals, ships, etc.

The basis of this training should be broad enough and the variety of materials available great enough to give every kind of talent an equal opportunity. Learning through direct experience rather than being taught creates discovery and rediscovery of methods. The teacher's ability will be shown in his knowledge of how to inspire and lead without domineering, when to show how to use a tool, such as a pocket-knife or a pair of scissors, and when to stand aside and allow the children to learn from their own self-guided efforts. He will know when the time has come to introduce new materials, new tools to fit the needs of the moment in a child's development, or when to organize a competition.

The small children work unrestrictedly; they are guided by their play instinct and by their curiosity to discover; they train their common sense in choosing the right materials—and they *do* choose the right materials! That is why we do not restrict small children in their choice of materials. They find out by trial and error certain laws as to what can be done with a certain material and what cannot be done. They find one cannot do everything with one material but only this or that. The unconscious forces are at work, as well as the ability to think. But the driving forces are intuition, imagination and fantasy. The constant training of all these forces is important in building up the future of a spiritually alive society.

We certainly do also draw, paint, print, but the pencil, colour and paper are only three media out of many hundreds. When children grow to about twelve years of age, they gradually discover different working processes, which may lead to the choice of new materials. *It will be discovered that material economy is important for a maximum of achievement with a minimum of effort.* It is not the quantity, but the quality of the result that counts. The question will arise—which materials suit one another? Does paper fit in with woodshavings? tin with straw? glass with sacking or plaster of Paris? wood with leather? and so on. The ten- to twelve-year-old children are already capable of thinking clearly and they ask themselves and decide what materials are best suited for making a face, an animal, a witch, a ship or an aeroplane.

We may then start with competitions, using only one material, or two, or three.

As you know, paper is generally used lying flat, but at Geelong Grammar School we try to use the paper standing upright as a fascinating building material. The edges are utilized and we may reinforce them by complicated folding. A technical problem will inevitably arise when we are confronted with the question of how to fasten materials so that the joins fit well and look well. Pasting and glueing should be used only in an emergency. Paper is usually pasted, but the children have to try to find other methods first, using their own inventive genius, such as folding, tying, pinning, sewing, etc. They will find their methods in different ways. After having tried all possible methods of fastening we may, of course, paste it. At the same time, we learn by experience the properties of the paper—its flexibility and rigidity, its potentialities in tensile strength, in tension and compression. Thus we train in constructive thinking, and with this endeavour to deal with vital problems of our present-day actualities.

Thus the child conquers his own world, he widens his knowledge by his self-guided efforts and he discovers the limitations of his own potentialities.

The study of materials in the senior school, as well as in adult classes, will always succeed, if begun with the basic impulse to play, and by experimenting. But in developing the course in the senior school we try to analyse materials and work in a more systematic way, guided by certain laws of our present-day form of achievement in modern architecture, interior decoration and household equipment. One of these characteristics is *economy of form*. This economy of form depends on the material and its function. The study and investigation of the *function* of a material is therefore naturally our first effort—which we call 'Study of Materials' (Pl. 2).

Craft education in our schools and industry, fairly similar, by the way, does consist chiefly in the teaching of established processes of

15 *The Dove flying from the Ark*
Janet Bolton (11), Firbank, Church of England Girls' Grammar
School, Sandringham, Victoria

Some authorities say that art is *not* a universal language
. . . But can anyone deny the universality of *child* art—
those paintings and drawings and modellings that stem
chiefly from the child's subconscious mind and instinct?
They have the marks of humanity. They arise from the
human desire to create and record. They demonstrate an
impulse that is subservient to neither race nor creed.
— John A. Campbell, *page 54*

16 *A Science Experiment*
Submitted for the Intermediate Certificate, New South Wales

treating raw materials, as the result of long technical development. The learning and application of these methods develop *skill* only, hardly any creative or imaginative potentialities. All these crafts are very useful indeed, but very limited in their practical aims—to produce well finished articles. Very often they are bad in proportion, in treatment, colour and decoration, thus diverging from certain important principles of our time. Our study of materials at Geelong is without the practical aim of producing household articles! It is often very difficult to introduce such studies and to convince teachers and parents that it is more important in school age to develop the creative and inventive abilities than to achieve skill. Crafts such as carpentry, bookbinding, leatherwork, metal work, pottery, etc., ought to be taught only when there are preliminary or parallel courses in the study of materials. Study of materials starts with undisturbed, uninfluenced and unprejudiced experiment and not, as in teaching of crafts, with one best method only. Free handling of materials without the practical aim of producing an article develops courage. At Geelong we do not start with a theoretical introduction, we start straight off with the materials.

We have seen that the study of materials does not aim at producing useful articles. Nevertheless, it *may* lead to the production of toys, as for example, a doll, or an aeroplane; or it may lead to group work, as in the making of a large relief map of the surrounding countryside of the country school, the farmhouses and paddocks with their fences, the trees and the bush—all with suitable materials, such as coloured sawdust, sand, sponges, sticks and wooden blocks pasted on. Different textures will be used for fields, ploughed land and grass paddocks as well as trees and houses. We have found in such projects that not only the children but the local farmers will come to school to see that their farms and paddocks are in the right spot.

In order to make sure of doing as much manual experimenting as possible, we restrict the use of tools at first. So, for instance, in clay work we start by using our hands only. What can we do with our hands, using every possible part of the hand in creating different surface textures—with the fingertips, nails, knuckles, the inside and outside of the hand? What happens if we push the clay with our nails? As the course advances, we make simple wooden tools, we use iron nails, brushes, buttons and combs, to find out what impressions can be made on clay, and we compare the surface textures

made by hand with those made with tools. We will find that some
of the surfaces already have the character of reliefs. What is a relief?
And many new problems open up a new world with interesting ideas—
such as comparisons of the relief qualities of architecture or furniture.

In the senior school we try to train ourselves in constructive thinking. These constructions must represent the functional qualities of
the material by fulfilling the technical requirements set forth in the
wording of the problem. Sometimes the results of these experiments
reveal new inventions of technical fittings. But even when we evolve
methods which are already known, we have discovered them in-
dependently through direct experience, and they are our own because
we have rediscovered them, and they have not been taught us. Certainly
this learning through experience takes more time than learning by
copying or being taught. But we learn by making mistakes; it sharpens
our criticism.

As the most essential aim of our teaching, however, is *economy,*
our basic criticism will be the ratio of the utmost *maximum of achievement to the utmost minimum of effort,* in materials as well as in labour.
And here again we strike the basic laws of form and their contemporary
interpretation. We distinguish between technical, economic and aesthetic considerations, between the static and the dynamic properties
of a material, of which the inherent characteristics determine the
way in which it can be used.

Textures. Study of *surface qualities,* or texture, is another method
of the study of form. It develops sensibility of the individual for the
aesthetic qualities of materials, and their relations to each other.
Experiments with surface textures are concerned with their appearance, rather than their inner qualities. Systematic scales of surface
textures, as, for example, from soft to hard, smooth to rough, warm
to cold, or polished to matt and dull, makes one sensitive to the
finest differences in touch and appearance. I quote here a few ex-
planations for certain classifications made by Joseph Albers, of the
Bauhaus, who is now art master of Blackmountain College in America:

We classify the appearance of the surface of a material as to structure,
facture and texture, which we differentiate carefully. These qualities of
surface can be combined and graduated somewhat, as colours are in
painting (hue, value, intensity).

Structure refers to those qualities of surface which reveal how the
raw material grows, or is formed, such as the grain of wood, or the
composite structure of granite.

Facture refers to those qualities of surface which reveal how the raw material has been treated technically, such as the hammered or polished surface of metal, or the wavy surface of corrugated paper.

Texture is a general term which refers to both 'structure' and 'facture' but only if both are present, for example the texture of polished wood reveals both the 'structure' (grain) and the 'facture' (polishing).

These surface qualities can be perceived usually by sight, and often by both sight and touch, for example the structure of highly polished wood can be perceived by eye but not by touch, the facture of a printed page can be perceived by sensitive fingertips, but not by the eye, etc.

Here are a few practical hints on how to organize work with materials. The very first objection to this work will be that it is practically impossible, because of lack of space in ordinary classrooms, and there are no extra rooms for arts and crafts. The answer is this: the study of materials *is* possible everywhere where there is a will and some courage to do it. We did this work (in Germany) in elementary classes of up to sixty children in one small classroom with the children in all elementary stages from six to fourteen years of age, squeezed together on long benches—in poor country schools without a penny for buying materials. The materials are collected by the children and the master, and stored in boxes labelled in large lettering. These boxes, wooden or cardboard, are best stored on low shelves along the side of the classroom, within easy reach of the children, or on tables. If there are no shelves or spare tables, they are just as well placed on the floor along a wall of the classroom. The boxes with materials are best grouped in systematic order, from soft to hard and, if possible, in two rows: (a) natural and raw materials, and (b) artificial and manufactured ones. The following materials are only suggestions—there are unlimited varieties of materials and countless ways of using them. Teachers will, of course, use mostly materials easily obtained; for example, if there is bush nearby, gum leaves, gum branches, bark, gum nuts, etc. If there is bamboo in the neighbourhood use bamboos. All these have unlimited possibilities.

(a) Natural and raw materials (from soft to hard): from raw wool, feathers, leather, raffia, straw, reeds, rushes, to soft shells (e.g. crayfish), woods, cork, bark, branches, acorns, pine cones, clay, sand, small stones.

(b) Artificial and manufactured materials: from cotton wool and woven materials of all kinds, cotton, linen, silk, to thread, string, card, paper, cardboard, corrugated cardboard, sawdust, woodshavings, linoleum, bakelite, prepared wood, such as dowelling and offcuts of all sizes, glass, wire and metal.

(c) Finished articles: match-boxes, cigarette packets, cotton reels, buttons, beads, milk bottle tops.

If we analyse most of our present art activities in schools, we find they are mainly based on the ideals of the Italian High Renaissance, five hundred years ago. But there is one remarkable difference. The artists of the fifteenth century worked, stimulated by the actualities of their times, with great enthusiasm, with a vital urge of curiosity, and the spirit of adventure. These impulses are replaced in our schools today by the attempt to teach established laws, such as the laws of perspective, etc., instead of studying these from the historical viewpoint only.

If we restrict ourselves to teaching established processes only, if we try to cram as much knowledge and skill as possible into the heads of pupils, teaching becomes truly a dull grind, and a very poor business. We must, as teachers and as pupils, learn from each other continually. Otherwise we will come to routine teaching, and a dead end.

I feel our art education must cope with the needs of both the present and later generations. Our future demands human beings who have the logical and truthfully working brain of an engineer and at the same time the soul and mind of an artist.

6

Art Education and the National Gallery of Victoria

SIR DARYL LINDSAY

Fifty years ago, except for the scholar, the student, and a sprinkling of the more enlightened public, art galleries and art museums the world over were not seriously considered as educational institutions. After the turn of the century the masses started to become aware of art; trustees, directors, and curators began to realize that they had a further responsibility other than the collecting and caring for works of art. They began to pull up their socks. As my friend Francis Taylor once said: 'The public have had their bellies full of prestige and pink marble, and want to know something about Art.'

The National Gallery of Victoria had no significance as a collection until the Felton Bequest came into operation in 1904. From then on great works of art were added to the collection, pictures, prints, etc. But it still had no coherence as a whole. It became a large collection with a sprinkling of a few dozen great pictures.

When I took over the direction in 1940 I was fortunate in having Sir Keith Murdoch—a man of great vision—as chairman. We decided to develop the collection so that it would have a definite educational value to the state and the whole of Australia. A new buying policy was adopted. The Italian, Flemish and Dutch, French and Spanish schools were built up. This was a start, but we were still lacking in a most important thing—the teaching of the history of fine art. Through the Melbourne *Herald*, Sir Keith Murdoch, always one to grasp at a new idea, founded the Chair of Fine Arts at the University of Melbourne.

Professor Burke's appointment to the post has shown splendid results in the few years he has been with us. His enthusiasm for his work, not only at the University but in the whole community, and his influence, have become national assets. Prior to Burke's appointment we were fortunate in getting the services of Dr Ursula Hoff, one of the finest scholars in this country, in order to develop and extend our print collection.

Up to this time we were getting little help from the Education Department, although we had developed a scheme for sending prints to schools. Through the co-operation of Mr Ramsay, Director of Education in Victoria, we were able to obtain the services of Mr Gordon Thomson from the Department as our Education Officer. He was later appointed Assistant Director.

All this helped to tie up the University, the Education Department, and the Gallery staff as a working team. I believe it has shown excellent results. In collaboration with the Education Department and with the help of Mr J. W. Mills we developed a scheme for making use of large coloured reproductions in the schools. The Department put up the money, and is half way to fulfilling its aim of thirty thousand prints for Victorian schools.

The travelling art exhibitions to country centres, developed by Mr. Thomson, have been a huge success, and have made the permanent appointment of an education officer necessary together with a permanent lecturer at the Gallery.

There is another point which I would like to mention here. Thirteen years ago there was no source of supply for trained gallery or museum personnel. Three galleries in Australia were without directors and no suitable men could be found. The jobs did not attract suitable people from overseas. It seemed to me that the National Gallery of Victoria collection with its large resources, and with the Felton Bequest behind it, was the natural place to train such people. An effort therefore was made to get cadets and train them at the Gallery, giving them time to take a course in Fine Arts at the University, but it failed. However, in spite of this, we were able to train two men who after a few years were able to take over the directorships of the Perth and Brisbane Galleries, and both are doing excellent jobs. But I still maintain that we should have cadets to train.

After my return from Europe in 1953 we revised and narrowed the overseas buying policy with the idea of strengthening certain existing schools and giving the collections generally a sounder educational value. This is being carried out and developed today.

Another activity we have developed is the *National Gallery Society* formed in 1947 with a membership of a few hundred. It now numbers over 1,800. Its objects are to foster an interest in the National Gallery and in the arts generally. Evening meetings are held in the Gallery each month throughout the year, most of them lectures connected with pictures and painters, or with ceramics, glass, furniture and other exhibits from the art museum. High quality musical programmes are also presented, sometimes in a specially arranged period setting, bringing all the arts into association. Four to five hundred members attend each meeting, often more than seats can be provided for, so that there is no doubt of the response to this approach. The society also sponsors special lecture courses, contributes to various activities, and is planning a series of art publications. Several individual members have also made generous gifts to the Gallery through the society. It has an office in the Gallery building, and of course depends upon the approval and co-operation of the Trustees and the Director, but it is financed by its members' subscriptions and is quite autonomous.

Guide lectures to metropolitan schools, loans to provincial galleries, loans to technical and high schools—these are some of the things we have attempted in using the Gallery collections for educational purposes. The ground has been cleared and the stage set, so to speak, and now the really difficult problems come up. We have the background, but how are we going to hand on the goods to others? How are we going to set about teaching this business of art? How are we going to give them something on which they can build their own standards of judgment and develop their taste? I am under no illusions about trying to put this across; it's a real snag. It is so easy to say what we have done, so easy to talk glibly about good and bad art. It gets us nowhere to tell people this is good art and that is bad art. At the most we express our opinion—and like parrots some may remember it. Half the time it goes in one ear—and comes out the same one. How are we going to make people *think* about art?

A course of Fine Arts, admirable as it is, will give the students the facts, but the facts are not enough. A student may know everything about the history of art, about all the great schools of painting and how they followed each other, and the individual painters who influenced the schools, and so on and so forth. They may end up knowing a great deal about art, but nothing whatever about drawing and painting. An attempt will have to be made to teach people about that intangible thing, taste; all the textbooks on art cannot teach taste. We have the ingredients for teaching, but no sure method of putting it across in large doses. We have our galleries of real works of art;

we have our teachers of fine arts; we have our painting and art schools; we have libraries of books on art; we have men and women who understand all these things, but to make the great mass of the people understand them is the problem. We have still got to make the student think for himself.

How can the student be made to think so that he can himself recognize, without being told, what is fine in art, what is first-rate, and what is perfection?

Sir Richard Winn Livingston, the great classical scholar and educationist, points out that a medical student will learn more, and recognize perfection, by seeing a great surgeon operate, than by reading all the textbooks in the world. It is the same with anything, you learn what is first-rate by contact with it. You learn what is first-rate in music by much listening. You learn what is first-rate in literature by much reading. You learn first-rate business methods by working in a first-rate business firm. You acquire good taste in wine by drinking good wine. And you learn what is first-rate in art by much looking and comparing. You won't get it out of books, or by looking at reproductions.

There are two ways in which we may help towards the understanding and the recognition of the first-rate in art. The first is that it is an excellent thing for children to be brought to galleries and for them to get the habit young of going to galleries, so that they will grow up in contact with the first-rate. Secondly, it's a good enough thing, I suppose, to let them make marks and play around with paints, like all normal young savages, provided they are not taught to be budding artists. If they are going to be artists, they will become artists, in spite of teaching. Playing with pencils and paints is a natural phase of a child's life, and should be considered and encouraged as such; but it should not be taken too seriously.

Art is a visual thing, something to look at, and the eye and mind should be trained to see and know its inner meaning, and it can be explained by people who know in simple terms. What applies to the child being brought up in close proximity to good art applies to the grown-up. It is by being brought into close contact with what is good over long periods that the intellect becomes trained and selective. The best that we can do is to supply this background; and the growing interest in art in Victoria today suggests that we are getting somewhere. But the ground as yet is only scratched.

7

Art and the Training of Teachers

GORDON THOMSON

One function of art education is to assist the child to mature and to help him, in the process, to enjoy creative experiences. A *second* is to provide him with ways of looking at his physical and social environment, a similar function to that of geography and physics on the one hand, and history and poetry on the other. A *third* function is to show him how to satisfy his instinctive aesthetic hungers and exercise his powers of qualitative judgment, having in mind that many more of the important decisions of life are made on considerations akin to aesthetic ones than is generally acknowledged. A *fourth* is to preserve and encourage his creative or inventive powers and a proper respect for these in others. *Lastly,* (in an educational world which has thrown out the classics and takes infinite pains to pre-digest all educational material to be immediately assimilable) education should give him an introduction to the mature art of his own culture. The study of classical literature did introduce to the child adult material of the highest quality. There is now a tendency, at least as far as the middle secondary level, to work only with toys. We should see to it that in art appreciation, at any rate, the child is introduced to adult culture. Otherwise, it would be possible for a child to leave school at fifteen or sixteen having met nothing that could possibly interest an adult, except some fragments of Shakespeare. It may be accepted that in a democracy a man has an absolute right of access to the culture of his own time and people.

I have set down these five functions because it seems to me that it is the job of teacher-training to perform them. The teachers' colleges have the difficult task of working at one remove from the material, but the place to examine teacher-training is in the ultimate result, the child's education. It has been agreed for long enough that art is not a technical or vocational subject, but forms part of a general education, and consequently it demands a high standard of general education of its teachers. It is to be deplored, particularly since art-teacher-training is highly specialized, that in some states lower standards of general education are accepted for admission to the service as art teachers than as teachers of other subjects.

Among the developments of recent times which have been fully applied in many schools with splendid results are the introduction of sculpture, the integration of arts and crafts, and the development of group activities. There has also, of course, been an enormous advance in the freedom with which paintings are made.

Some modern developments, however, which have not been sufficiently examined in Australian schools, are the study of materials in the tradition of the Bauhaus (which, except for one or two schools, seems to have been completely misunderstood or neglected), and the co-operation of art teachers with psychologists. Some of the crafts, notably woodwork, are well-advanced so far as technique is concerned but very much out of date in their function of exercising students in modern design.

The Bristol Report suggests that the general condition operating in many countries is a firm opposition by the older (and often controlling) teachers to the application of advanced methods and principles. This is bound to obtain since there has been such sudden and radical change in attitudes to art education in recent years.

One of the weaknesses of teacher-training is that it is available only to the immature. When young teachers leave training, and it is fair to say that teachers have never been better equipped or more enthusiastic for their work, they may meet immediately two conditions which may neutralize their training. The first of these is the syllabus, or, as it is sometimes feelingly called, 'The Curse of Study'. In at least one important division of the system in Victoria this is very much behind the times, not having liberated itself from either the *Ecole Polytechnique* (whence its rigidly rationalistic procedure and geometry), or from the arts and crafts movement (whence its austere craft disciplines and insistence on the value of repetitive ornament).

While it is true that in many cases the teacher is given a free hand to deviate from and interpret this syllabus in order to make the fullest use of his training, unfortunately there are many cases where he is frustrated by head teachers or district inspectors.

It is unfair to expect a senior teacher to distinguish between the mistakes and follies of inexperience and recently accepted educational practice differently aimed from that sanctioned by his training. However extensive his course in drawing from a flat example and decorative design in three colours from a flowering plant, it cannot help him to decide whether the educational results of tower-building in straws, razor-blades and corrugated board justify the disturbance. It is proper under the circumstances for him to forbid the practice, because it is he who is responsible, but it defeats modern teacher-training.

The great majority of children in Victorian primary schools are offered no alternative to that dirty, unresponsive and difficult medium, the cheap pastel. My own child, after a joyous period in the kindergarten with paints and large paper, has to settle down to the diligent production of neat shapes drawn from a template on small paper, and coloured with his choice of two colours. He has been taught at seven years that it is wrong to leave a space between the earth and the sky, and that black is a 'dirty' colour. Now all of this cuts directly across teachers' college training. And it is important if this training is not to be frustrated that inspectors and headmasters should be equipped to demand something better than such teaching.[1]

There is a clear case for short intensive courses for senior personnel in the visual arts and the educational principles involved in their use in schools. This would enable their valuable experience to be put behind, instead of against, developments in art education. Syllabus changes would not then be long delayed.

It is necessary, in the training of teachers, to make them aware of the special problems of the Australian country town. There, the art teacher will find himself one of the few active proponents of civilization. People are always anxious to learn, despite appearances to the contrary. There is the story of the scientific farmer, who found that the only way he could interest his neighbours in his experimental plots was to put an eight foot fence around them. They then stealthily copied his methods. What the teacher does will influence people more than what he says. If he talks of the great value of art and buys the cheapest pictures and the best cricket bats; if instead of finding a first-class artist to design the school badge, he allows a senior student

---

[1] Some important recent developments in Victorian primary schools raise hopes that these criticisms will soon be invalidated.

to perpetrate one of those shields with tangled letters; it is on these things that the country boy will form his estimate of the status of art.

The critical point of this problem is how the teacher approaches contemporary art, and whether he can invest it with any meaning which the pupils can relate to their already established values. If it clearly has significance for the teacher himself it will help more than anything else. To this end he should maintain his own creative practice wherever possible.

The status of the visual arts within the school is not high. The Psychology Department at the University of Melbourne often asks boys to rank subjects in order of preference. Art or one of the crafts usually comes first. Then they ask them to rank the subjects in order of their importance. Art invariably comes last. I am interested to learn from the Bristol Report that this is not a local condition, but widespread. What can be done to raise the status of the visual arts?

I suppose it is well known that we are fortunate enough to have at our University a School of Fine Arts. If a list of its contributions to art education were compiled it would be very impressive indeed. Not the least of these is that it forms a rallying point for the visual arts inside an academic and technical stronghold, and has helped enormously to improve the status and the public relations of art. Establishment of such schools in other states is an obvious first step.

The second is more complicated. There is always a good case for prerequisites and obligatory subject-linkages. But they are an arbitrary specializing force which creates much havoc in education, and some of the status inferiority of the visual arts has been caused by the masters of academic subjects saying 'You can't do this unless you do this too!' But the demand for freedom is strong and this sort of thing is disappearing. The time must surely come when subjects will be given standing according to the time spent in their study and the cultural level reached, and not according to their value as preparation for the University.

I should like to see a course devised which would give opportunities for subject-combinations selected from both university and art-teacher-training study. It is desirable, and would eventuate in nearly every case, that an art teacher should study crafts also, but an occasional one would prefer not to submerge an interest in, say, a language. Let us not presume that all good art teachers are of the same kind.

This interchange would involve recognition by the University of art subjects, and the establishment of courses of equal duration for all secondary teachers, but these are not extravagant demands. Herbert Read says: 'It should be one hierarchy related to one system of training, and providing within its limits the possibilities of promotion and development which should be characteristic of all democratic institutions', and quotes Whitehead on the question of separate specialized training: 'Both types (the gross specialised values of the merely practical man and the thin specialised values of the mere scholar) have missed something and if you add together the two sets of values you do not obtain the missing elements.'[2]

You will see that I propose identical qualifications for all secondary teachers. Apart from raising the general status of art in education, there would be other important results of this. In Victoria, art teachers' qualifications do not admit them to the School of Education. The establishment of identical qualifications would remove this disability, which at present partly accounts for the meagreness of investigation and publication in our field. Recent history shows that art education has contributions to make to general pedagogics. And several important questions await investigation here, including the application of the Loewenfeld haptic-visual separation to Australian children. Education courses would equip and stimulate art teachers for such activities. The prestige of the School of Education qualification is high, and the acquisition of its qualifications by art teachers would result in more of the higher posts, as principals and administrators, being open to them. This is not without effect on the status and efficiency of the subject.

In a subject which needs it more than others, there is disappointingly little international interchange. Not even senior inspectors in the Victorian system have been sent abroad to study recent developments, and our art ideas suffer from in-breeding. I know of only one teachers' college art lecturer who has travelled abroad, and he in 1938. And visitors here since 1937 have been very few. I should like to urge that the authorities be asked to examine the possibility of sending senior teacher-training personnel abroad as often as University professors are expected to travel, of inviting eminent authorities in art education for courses of lectures, and of widening the range of travelling scholarships available to art teachers to at least that of other students.

2 H. Read, *Education through Art* (Faber and Faber, London, 1949), p. 254.

8

An Experiment with Art in Adult Education

COLIN BADGER

There is a great diversity of opinion about the scope and method of adult education among those actively engaged in it as teachers or administrators, the principal point at issue being the question of intensive or extensive practice. In view of the extremely limited resources at the disposal of the Australian systems, it is held by some that the most effective way of using such resources is to attempt a thorough-going education for a few people, at something approaching university level, and by others, that adult education is best organized so as to attract a large audience, with a definitely popular appeal and, if needs be, a somewhat superficial content. This is hardly the place to set out the arguments for and against these rival policies, but it should be said, at the outset, that the writer's experience and conviction is that in the Australian context, it is the popular approach to adult education which is the most practicable and the most rewarding. What follows in this paper is an attempt to describe the effort of the Victorian Council of Adult Education to interest the Victorian public in art and it is not an attempt either to lay down general principles on the subject or to set out desirable aims and objectives in theory.

The Victorian Council of Adult Education is a statutory body, with definite functions laid down in the Adult Education Act of 1946. It began active work in 1947, with a background of experience and effort derived from the University Extension-W.E.A. set-up which was the main form of Australian adult education until the post-war period. The Council derives the major part of its fund from state government grants. It has no direct association with the University and is not formally part of the State Education Department, although it is responsible to Parliament through the Minister of Education and reports annually to Parliament through the minister. In its short history in Victoria, it has succeeded in making a fairly marked impact upon the social and cultural life of the state. It has established good working relations with the major cultural and educational organizations and operates with the maximum of freedom and minimum of interference.

The Council's policy is best described as being that of providing a service for those who may wish or can be encouraged to continue their education into adult life. Its programme falls under three headings: first, organization of evening classes in the Melbourne area, of which some ninety are arranged each year, running in series of ten or twenty lectures, on a great variety of subjects—current enrolment is about 4,700. Second, the organization of a service for small groups (ten to fifteen people) in city and country centres, based upon the regular supply of prepared material (books, pamphlets, records, plays, art material etc.) and of a service for existing local organizations of many kinds. There are approximately 370 groups and organizations using this service. Third, the 'extensive' work, predominantly in the country, which consists of the organization of regular tours by professional musicians, actors and other artists, giving 'one night' performances in country towns on a defined circuit, which includes more than 120 towns.

The Council has not attempted to build up an adult education organization as such. It tries to work through and with existing organizations, helping them in ways suggested by their own needs, but not seeking to impose any special pattern. It has been successful, for example, in stimulating a very active interest in the theatre in Victoria through the Travelling Theatre with the result that there is now a flourishing network of dramatic societies in Victoria, affiliated, not with the C.A.E., but with the voluntary organization, the Victorian Drama League.

It is within this general pattern that the C.A.E. work in the field of art is to be considered. At each stage and in each section of the work some attention is given to the subject of the visual arts, with a strong emphasis upon the idea of eventual participation and the widening of the influence of art in daily life. Courses on the history of art, on art appreciation and aesthetics are a regular feature of the city and suburban classes and two or three such classes are arranged each year. These are planned so as to offer courses which are primarily popular and introductory and others which imply a considerable knowledge of the subject and which take up special periods and painters. An effort is made to provide variety, by offering courses in which a number of lecturers are invited to take part, lecturing on their special subject.

At the same time, practical painting classes are arranged. These have been a feature of C.A.E. work for some years and are highly popular. The classes are under the direction of one teacher, with an elementary and advanced class in the city each year, together with one or two suburban classes. Members of the classes are encouraged to join the voluntary Adult Education Association painting group, which works throughout the year, arranging week-end schools, visits to the National Gallery, sketching and painting excursions and so on.

A good deal of thought and effort has been put into the development of interest in art in country centres and the main phases of this effort are so arranged as to lead to a consistent plan. The central feature is the travelling exhibition which is a joint venture of the C.A.E. and the National Gallery; the C.A.E. provides the organizing framework and the Gallery the material and special services. The travelling exhibition consists of a set of well-planned screens, which are readily transportable, carried in a special vehicle, on which the pictures can be carried and shown with a minimum of difficulty, and without much risk (Pl. 14). Arrangements for each tour of the exhibition are made by the Council, which provides publicity material (window cards, press blocks, pars, leaflets, etc.) and the necessary local contacts.

Exhibitions are changed year by year, a 'tour' lasting roughly twenty to thirty weeks and covering a large part of the state. The general rule is for a formal 'opening' in each town, followed by a lecture, given by the Education Officer of the National Gallery, together with guide lectures to parties from the schools. The exhibition remains in each town for a period, determined largely by the size of the population and the local interest, varying from three or four days up to a week. Catalogues are sold, but the exhibition is otherwise free and costs are shared between the Council and the National Gallery. In recent years, it has been the practice to arrange for the showing of 16mm. films on art, as an added interest feature.

The purpose of the exhibition is twofold. First, to make known the work of the Gallery to a wider public and to demonstrate that the Gallery is in fact the National Gallery of Victoria and not merely of Melbourne; secondly, to encourage local and individual interest in painting, in the hope that local study groups, practical painting classes, local exhibitions, or even a local gallery may be established.

17　*Bush Picnic*
Yvonne Chick (15), Katoomba High School, New South Wales

18 Loading screens and poles into the Travelling Exhibition Unit, a joint venture of the National Gallery and the Council of Adult Education, Victoria

Travelling exhibitions of original works of art from a National Gallery to country centres were begun in Australia by the National Gallery of New South Wales in 1944 and continued, with a break during 1948-50, until 1954 when they were, unfortunately, abandoned. A travelling exhibition scheme operated jointly by the Council of Adult Education and the National Gallery of Victoria was begun in 1948, and has continued to provide a splendid educational service to Victorian rural communities ever since — *See page 50*

For this reason, at the time when the exhibition was planned, the Council also began to build up its collection of prints, slides, books and study material for the Discussion Group Service and used the catalogue of the exhibition to draw attention to the fact that this material was available to those whose appetite had become whetted by a visit to the exhibition. There has been a rapid development in the art groups served by the Discussion Group Service. There are at present some 150 groups including, apart from art groups, literature, drama and music groups and many clubs and other organizations which draw upon the art material. The Council now has good 35mm. slides, 1,900 prints and a large collection of books.

Several discernible results from the travelling exhibition may be noted. The first, the growth of art discussion groups in country areas, has already been noted. The second, the organization of local art exhibitions, has been important and may well be a pointer to the future. The first local exhibition was held at St Arnaud, followed fairly quickly by others at Maryborough, Swan Hill and Sale. These were exhibitions of pictures locally owned, rather than of pictures locally painted, but in the subsequent exhibition at Maryborough, the emphasis was upon local production. Exhibitions of the latter kind, which have aroused great local interest, have been held at Sale, Warragul and at Traralgon, Birchip and Portland, where there are groups of painters at work.

In 1953 the C.A.E., with the help of an advisory committee, thought that the time was ripe to organize an Art from the Country Exhibition in Melbourne. One hundred and sixty entries were received for this and the exhibition surprised both the organizers and the critics by the number and the quality of the work received. This exhibition is now held biennially, and has become an interesting feature of Melbourne's art activities.

While anxious to do everything possible to encourage country painters and artists, the Council is unable to go far, since the cost of sending tutors and instructors to country centres is heavy. At most, all that can be afforded is the occasional lecture-demonstration or tutor's visit. To some extent, this deficiency is remedied by the Annual Summer School, held at the National Art Gallery arranged by the Council, which offers an opportunity for some 150 people to take part in an intensive ten-day residential school, with ample facilities for practical work. It would be difficult to over-estimate the value of the summer school in stimulating interest in art and in providing at least an elementary introduction to practice. From the school each year a group of enthusiasts go out who carry on the good work in their own districts and it is from these 'carriers', so to speak, that the novel ventures in country towns take their point of departure.

A strong effort is being made in Victoria to encourage the provision of a programme which will include all the arts. A great deal of effort, in recent years, has been put into the development of the idea of local festivals as part of the yearly work of art clubs. Several of these are now by way of being regarded as annual features and two—Maryborough and Wangaratta festivals—have been conspicuously successful. At Maryborough, a purely local exhibition was arranged in conjunction with the festival and was largely attended. At Wangaratta, the travelling exhibition was on display for the period, with lectures on the exhibition, guide lectures for schools and films, organized as part of the programme. A recent innovation has been the organization of a Gippsland regional exhibition, as part of the one-act play festival at Traralgon. This exhibition, opened by a leading Melbourne critic, ran for a full week and was seen, it is estimated, by 1,500 people. The idea has now been passed on to Bordertown and an art exhibition is held in conjunction with the Bordertown Drama Festival in August each year.

The policy of the Council in the matter is readily outlined. It is to try, as far as possible (1) to have at least one group, however small, in each town organized for the purpose of the study of art; (2) to use the interest thus created to assist in the publicity and organization of the art exhibition tour and to follow the tour by further discussion and the creation of a desire for further such exhibitions, organized, if possible, on a local basis; (3) to stimulate the kind of interest which leads to the practical participation of individuals as artists and to create an environment in which their work may be encouraged and understood; (4) to encourage, wherever possible, the formation of regional galleries. It is hoped, eventually, to set up regional galleries, not necessarily for the purchase and showing of standard works of art, but for the presentation of regional and local pictures.

The Council's efforts in the art field have been strenuous and have meant a great deal of work and time. The results, to date, though not spectacular, are encouraging. It is believed that the underlying policy is sound, and that with persistent work much can be done to educate and enliven the taste of a very wide section of the public. Co-operation with the National Gallery, close collaboration with the schools, active encouragement of local government agencies and business enterprises, immediate response to the first signs of interest among individuals and groups are all important elements in the policy and the Council is fully aware of them.

Among the projects which are regarded as highly desirable, but which the Council has not yet been able to organize are (1) a series of visits to provincial galleries with guide lectures, on a 'short term' basis; (2) a travelling exhibition of modern furniture and decor; (3) exhibitions in country centres of handcraft and pottery.

Art classes arranged at Pentridge gaol (Pl. 23) have shown interesting results, but these classes are regarded as having a therapeutic and remedial aspect, rather than a purely artistic interest.

9

Art and International Understanding

A Report on the Bristol Seminar on Art Education

JOHN A. CAMPBELL

The importance of graphic expression in the young child before he
has acquired mastery over the more complex literary form needs
no comment. His drawings and paintings are a simple, natural, permanent means of communication and he uses it as such, naïvely and
innocently. For those who wish to read it, a child's drawing gives
deeper access to his thoughts and feelings than any other expression
and it is indeed the fortunate parent or teacher who has not forgotten
that language or who has been able to re-learn it.

Some authorities say that art is *not* a universal language. They
have various and substantial reasons. But can anyone deny the universality of *child* art—those paintings and drawings and modellings
that stem chiefly from the child's subconscious mind and instinct?
They have the marks of humanity. They arise from the human desire
to create and record. They demonstrate an impulse that is subservient
to neither race nor creed.

In a child's art we see universal aspects of his physiological and
psychological make-up expressed intuitively and in his own childlike
way before he is consciously aware of (or prepared to react to) the
limitations of the adult form of life and the intellectual and rational
criteria of his adult society. To those who understand the language of
child art there is no doubt as to the universality of that language.

UNESCO and the national agencies of that organization are fully
aware of the suitability of art, and of child art in particular, as a
means of displaying the 'other point of view'. International exhibitions
of both have already contributed to a fulfilment of their aims and it
has been noticeable that in all such exhibitions of children's art, even

54

in those including the Art of Youth, there is an underlying similarity despite apparent national differences.

The symposium *Education and Art* is a direct result of the Bristol Seminar. Teachers are always accused of 'talking shop'; art teachers particularly must confess to it. The common problems, trials and triumphs attributable to art education and shared by both child and teacher or anyone else concerned with the practice of child art, bring about an epidemic of happy enthusiasm. It was this infectious enthusiasm almost approaching a spiritual elation which pervaded the Bristol international gathering of art educationists. The physical handicap of spoken and written languages, and of racial differences, simply disappeared before the all-sufficing satisfaction of comparing notes in the common idiom of child art. Long before group discussions, even before the first general session, almost in the first half-hour of meeting one another, the participants sensed a sympathy and 'oneness' and an eagerness to 'talk shop'. They were simply unaware of racial differences.

Undoubtedly the Bristol Seminar on Art Education was by no means unique in this direction. Other meetings of specialists have had the same experience and along these lines of conference at least UN is finding satisfactory vehicles for international understanding.

Despite a rather pessimistic note from Jean Thomas from the UNESCO Secretariat concerning financial support, the Bristol participants were determined to attempt something tangible at an international level to foster art education. An Institute of Art Education was suggested. Exchange of art exhibitions, publications, films, teachers, students, etc., through UNESCO as a clearing house, was to be developed. A temporary committee for the preparatory stages of setting up an International Society for Education through Art was formed. A constitution for INSEA (International Society for Education through Art) has been established. This organization can mean a great deal to art educationists the world over. The following inaugural resolution[1] was adopted:

The Members of the International Society for Education through Art believing:

that *art* is one of man's highest forms of expression and communication;

that *creative activity* in art is a basic need common to all people;

[1] *Education and Art* (UNESCO, Paris, 1954), p. 120.

that *education through art* is a natural means of learning at all periods of the development of the individual, fostering values and disciplines essential for full intellectual, emotional and social development of human beings in a community;

that *association* on a world-wide basis of those concerned with education through art is necessary in order that they may share experiences, improve practices and strengthen the position of art in relation to all education;

that *co-operation* with those concerned in other disciplines of study and domains of education would be of mutual advantage in securing closer co-ordination of activities directed to solving problems in common;

that *international understanding* would benefit from a more completely integrated design and permanent structure, for the diffusion of beliefs and practices concerning education through art, so that the right man 'freely to participate in the cultural life of the community, to enjoy the arts' and to create beauty for himself in reciprocal relationship with his environment, would become a living reality;

resolve

'to support an international society for education through art in accordance with the foregoing statement of principles and beliefs, with a duly adopted Constitution and Rules, and to accept for Membership in the Society those individuals and organizations that shall undertake to abide by the Constitution and Rules of the Society.'

10

Art for the Living

HAL MISSINGHAM

One of the more obvious sicknesses of our present civilization is the divorce of the arts from the everyday life of man. Art cannot be considered an extraneous activity, it must be regarded as an absolute necessity if we are to function properly as human beings. When we are deprived of it we sicken. During the last war, when the energies of millions were pressed into inhumanly destroying one another, a clamour for participation in the arts welled and strengthened day by day as the physical pressure grew greater and more intolerable.

When we consider the succession of fierce and decimating wars of the last four hundred years, the phrase 'international understanding' seems an odd conceit. That it should be mentioned at all is a hopeful augury that it can be brought about, and that in bringing it to man's consciousness art should be indicated as a common meeting ground is even more a cheering sign.

This common meeting ground will not need to be long delayed. Mankind is in a parlous state of fear and indecision. In five hundred years we have developed our physical resources out of all knowledge and at a steadily increasing momentum.

We have improved our working conditions and increased our leisure, but we have little idea of what to do with this leisure. There exists little to occupy our released energies in a constructive way, in a manner which will develop us as human beings. When we leave our work the choice of constructive relaxation lies, in the main, in going to the races, to football, to cricket, or to the seaside. If we are not interested in physical effort we listen to the radio, turn on television, or visit the cinema.

There has been in our education singularly little to prepare us otherwise; the state does not provide facilities to keep us mentally healthy. We have the curious spectacle of mentally ill people being treated to doses of the arts to effect their cure, when these same arts, if fostered, developed and available in a community, would have prevented their being in hospital at all.

It is only recently that a large proportion of mankind has become educated, only recently that we have arrived at a stage when we can read the daily newspaper, the comic-strip, the sporting results and the latest details of murder and rape. We are educated to the point where we can calculate the odds at racecourses and in football pools with astonishing aptitude and accuracy, and in many other remarkable skills.

In education in its deeper sense, in education for our place as humans amongst other humans, we are practically illiterate. Our twenty-four hour day is now divided roughly into three equal periods. Eight hours of troubled sleep prepares us for eight hours' work, and another eight hours in which to disport ourselves. We are reasonably educated in the first two and, as I say, practically illiterate in the third. I take this in great measure to be largely the fault of an educational system which does not prepare us in any way to make use of our leisure, or provide facilities so that we may help ourselves.

Almost all the education we receive after adolescence is second-hand. We become non-participants in life and the deep and abiding experiences which constitute a full life. We take our love vicariously from the reigning movie stars, according to our sex; our sport from the edge of the arena, often not as close as this, but from the loudspeaker of our radio and the image on the television screen.

Our experiences of music are quite removed from direct contact with the original. Firstly, by the music being recorded mechanically on to a disc, then by this disc being played, also mechanically (by a euphemistically-named 'disc-jockey') and finally by the barrier of a radio set, which is often quite incapable of reproducing the limited sound waves which reach it from a central broadcasting station. To millions of human beings this sound *is* music.

Our education in art is equally remote and second-hand. Reproductions of original art are today being manufactured by the hundred million, some shockingly bad, some so finely printed that it is difficult to tell them from the original (the maker's claim—not mine). If these are properly framed so that the paper on which they are printed is hidden, you just can't tell the difference! As a consequence these reproductions are so expensive that only the more affluent of the educated can afford the luxury of the possession of this second-hand art. Those who own, at such remove, the works of El Greco, Van Gogh, Picasso and Toulouse-Lautrec are vociferous in setting themselves up as connoisseurs before their less well endowed neighbours. It hardly occurs to them to purchase an original work of art. Reproductions *are* their originals.

Education should prepare any human being to share his deepest experiences with his fellow man everywhere, regardless of colour, race, or creed. It is an astonishing thing that it grows more and more difficult to make such contacts. Governments and rulers place greater and greater restraints on exit and entry permits, on how much currency may be used by any of us should we be foolish enough to desire such contact with our fellows; and all the time that visas are being scanned, passports withheld and currency refused, a long-drawn lip-service cry of 'international understanding' goes echoing around the world.

What does understanding mean? It is not a question of languages, or literature, or art, although all these are helpful adjuncts. It is the undoubted fact that human beings if constantly in contact and left to themselves will delight in discovering the beauties and absurdities in each others' characters. It seems of singularly little use constantly to abjure us to enjoy such an understanding when the first requirements are so desperately hard to come by. We no longer belong to local groups and isolated communities as did previous civilizations. We belong to all mankind: education *must* be directed so that we *may* belong. A vital change in education of this kind would make international understanding a much closer reality. We need desperately to accept our civilization and to identify ourselves with it if we are to survive. We need desperately to enjoy the arts of our fellow humans.

International understanding may profitably employ the arts as a significant part in the plan to bring people into harmonious relationships. In such use governments must provide facilities to enable these relationships to cement together. When I say that governments must provide, I do so advisedly because of the commonly held belief that we should pay for such services. The phrase 'Let people pay or they won't appreciate it' is heard all too frequently. In point of fact we *do* pay a colossal sum of money every second of every year just to be allowed to exist. We most certainly subscribe enough to warrant participation in the arts as our just right.

Galleries displaying the visual arts should be accessible continuously, seven days a week and at night. There should be exhibition space available where the achievements of our own artists could be seen. Without doing so we cannot share the profound contact with the universe which they enjoy. There must also be facilities for those millions of people who live at a distance from their fellows.

We should give up as useless the idea that we should only be allowed to share in the arts of past civilizations. Unless we believe in our own arts, and can participate freely in them, fewer and fewer people will become sensitive to these arts and there will be less and less demand for the deeper experiences. Then we shall indeed go down under a spiritual malnutrition. Art is a living thing; not to be denied, entering in some measure and some degree into the lives of every one of us minute by minute, day by day, year in and year out. A painting is not something done and finished with, hung on the wall, forgotten and immediately dead. It lives constantly in each person who looks at it and receives or rejects what it has to offer. From the arts we take the spiritual food necessary to us as our tastes and needs develop and change.

I think we must reiterate at every possible moment that art is a man-made activity, not a natural phenomenon. The ability to practise and enjoy art is one of the significant attributes which most strongly differentiates us from all other forms of life, and is common and creative in every one of us in some form or another. We may not all be first-rate executants but we can, and needs must, participate according to our necessities.

All art is an attempt by man to impose an order on the elemental chaos which surrounds him. The artist discovers and presents a specific form and pattern. This war against terror and darkness is never won, the necessities of the human spirit requiring first one form-pattern and then another as its awareness grows or declines. I believe that we have never at any time been more receptive to the deep need for international understanding, that we have great artists of all kinds working amongst us, equal in every way to the great ones of past eras, and that mankind is capable of tremendous things, both physically and spiritually. All art is educational and international, willy-nilly, if we accept education as meaning the development of *man:* an integration of the mental, emotional and scientific responses which make him unique.

I I

The 1959 Art Syllabus for Victorian Secondary Schools

In recent years secondary art education in Victoria has undergone a fundamental transformation. As late as 1947 the syllabus stressed the acquisition of certain types of skill, took no regard for the personal needs of individual pupils, made very little provision for imaginative expression, and there was little attempt to stimulate the pupil's creative powers.

When Joseph Burke arrived from England in 1947, to become the first *Herald* Professor of Fine Arts in the University of Melbourne, a movement for reform in art education in Victoria was already under way among art teachers. His appointment, however, gave an added weight and authority to that movement and made it possible to institute a new approach to art teaching in the secondary schools, to improve methods of training art teachers, and to introduce art as a matriculation subject. In recent years the educational status of the subject has improved greatly in Victoria.

Under Professor Burke's chairmanship a syllabus sub-committee of the Arts and Crafts Standing Committee of the Schools Board, University of Melbourne, made extensive enquiries from August to December 1948, into the teaching of art in Victorian secondary schools. Evidence was taken from a wide range of authoritative opinion both within and outside Australia concerning the educational value of the art syllabus then in existence. Written evidence was taken, for example, from such people as Sir Herbert Read, author of *Education through Art*, Mr Clifford Ellis, principal of Corsham Court, Wiltshire, and Mr Wilfred Blunt, drawing master at Eton College; and in Australia from Mrs A. P. Derham, art mistress at the Victorian Kindergarten Training College, Professor O. A. Oeser, Professor of Psychology, University of Melbourne, Dr L. Hirschfeld Mack, art master at

Geelong Grammar School, and Mr George Bell. Verbal evidence was also taken from a wide group of art teachers, artists, etc. The weight of opinion was overwhelmingly in favour of a drastic revision of the syllabus to bring it more into line with contemporary thought on art education. It was widely agreed that the then existing syllabus was designed neither to stimulate creative activity nor to provide a foundation for the development of good taste. It was felt that too much time was given to rote learning in the appreciation section of the syllabus, and that there was insufficient attention given to the work of contemporary artists. In the study of architecture emphasis lay upon the study of ornament rather than upon essential construction.

Most of the authorities consulted were of the opinion that art examinations should be abolished, attention being drawn to the effect of examinations upon teaching such as: close attention to superficial finish, extensive note taking, insincerity, excessive factual details, etc. Examinations, it was pointed out, are anxiety-producing phenomena which set up conditions inimical to artistic production. It was also claimed that examination methods are not successful in predicting further success or in recognizing desirable educational results.

In the light of the recommendations of the sub-committee new courses of study in art were introduced into Victorian secondary schools in 1952. These courses implemented many of the changes recommended by the witnesses interviewed. It was felt, however, at the time, that since so many art teachers had been trained in the older methods of teaching, the new course should be to some extent transitional, and form a bridge between the old and the new approach.

The new 'transitional' course, as we may call it, operated within a period of active discussion concerning art education in Victoria which was carried on, notably, in the Refresher School for Teachers of Arts and Crafts, 1949, and the Art Teachers' Seminar, 1953, organized by the Department of Education and the Fine Arts Department, University of Melbourne; the UNESCO Seminar, 1954; and the Art Seminar for Secondary and Technical School Teachers, 1956, held at Mac-Robertson Girls' High School, Melbourne.

By 1957 many teachers felt that the time had come for a further re-assessment of the position. The continuous activity and discussion of the Art Teachers' Association of Victoria, founded in 1953, played a most active part in this movement for further reform. Accordingly, a sub-committee of the Arts and Crafts Standing Committee of the Schools Board met from August to November 1957 and drafted a new course of study which was subsequently adopted by the Schools Board.

The new syllabus seeks to eliminate certain weaknesses which have revealed themselves in the operation of the 'transitional' syllabus. It seeks, for example, to integrate all sections of the course more closely than hitherto, so that activity in imaginative expression, observational drawing, and design may proceed in a unified fashion. The section on appreciation and taste, likewise, has been related more closely to the practical sections of the syllabus. Emphasis has been placed upon the need to obtain a wide knowledge of the many art-forms which man has evolved during his long history, not by rote learning, but by means of a direct visual study of many masterpieces.

No syllabus can be perfect; and it is to the teaching rather than to the courses of study that we must turn for the real results. This syllabus, like its predecessor, may be regarded as transitional, for any syllabus that remains static will soon lose its life and vitality. Nevertheless, it is confidently believed that it contains a balanced course of study in keeping with the new spirit and philosophy of art education. It will be found that much of what has been recommended in the papers in earlier sections of this book has found a worthy place in the new curriculum.

THE SYLLABUS

The aim of the course. The aim of the course is to develop the creative imagination of the pupil, to foster a lively and intelligent interest in art in everyday life, and to raise the standard of public taste. Above all else the art lesson should stimulate the pupil's sense of wonder and enjoyment of the world about him, while at the same time seeking to develop his inner emotional life and latent powers of imagination.

Successful teaching in the course will preserve the pupil's joy and satisfaction in creative activities while at the same time developing a more mature approach (both to subject matter and the technical resources at the pupil's disposal) suited to early adolescence.

The art room. The following suggestions are inserted as a guide to art teachers who are planning new art rooms or refurnishing old ones. The room should be spacious and possess good light, and a supply of water. A smooth floor surface, preferably covered with linoleum, will greatly facilitate cleaning. Movable furniture is essential. Desks should be flat-topped to enable them to be moved together to make larger table units for group work. A number of adjustable easels should be provided. There should be ample cupboard space around the room, folio-racks, display boards, and, wherever possible, a store-room attached to the art room. Flat drawers will be needed for storing paper, bins for storing material used in three-dimensional work. It should be possible to darken the art room quickly for the purpose of showing slides. Every art room should be provided with its own projector.

The use of materials. Pupils should be given every opportunity to experiment with a wide variety of materials. Only in this way will they best be able to develop modes of creative expression suited to their interests and personalities. Confronted with a new material a pupil often experiences a sense of discovery and develops new powers of personal expression.

The approach to style. Not all creative ability in the visual arts expresses itself in realistic forms. Allowance must always be made for widely varied forms of creative activity. It is recognized that different teachers have different methods, and a rich variety of approach is to be encouraged. Forms of expression experimented with might range from realistic methods to highly personal and abstract interpretations of experience. Pupils, for instance, may be encouraged to translate their reactions to music in visual forms by means of any suitable media. In every case form should arise in response to the work being done rather than be imposed upon it, the aim being always to assist the pupils towards a type of expression congenial to them.

The approach to subject matter. The teacher must always be ready to suggest interesting and stimulating topics suitable to the age and emotional experience of the pupils. At times topics will be suggested by the corporate activities and interests in which teachers and pupils share alike. At times two or three topics will be found more stimulating than one. But the lesson should never become merely 'do what you like'. It is to be remembered, furthermore, that when pupils enter the secondary school they are boys and girls; when they leave it they are, or they soon will be, young men and women. The art course, therefore, must be related to the rapid physical, emotional, intellectual and imaginative development of the normal child passing through adolescence. It is just as important to avoid trivial subject matter which holds no genuine appeal for young adolescents as it is to avoid insistence upon a particular style of working. Teachers should also learn to distinguish between the personal images which proceed from a healthy and vigorous imagination and the stereotyped images which indicate an impoverished emotional life. To quote Henri Matisse: 'The cinema, posters and magazines present us every day with a flood of ready-made images which are to the eye what prejudices are to the mind.' A good deal of use should be made of subjects drawn from the pupil's direct experience of life: the home, the school, and the school district.

The individual and the group. While every endeavour should always be made to safeguard the individual interests of each child, experienced teachers have found that pupils enjoy working as a class, or in class groups, especially in the earlier years of the secondary school. It is important, therefore, to develop this enjoyment of corporate activity, and for the teacher to become a part of it. In the higher grades pupils whose technical knowledge of materials and powers of imagination and observation have developed will often work quite well and happily as individuals, but even then they should never be separated from the satisfaction and confidence that come from being part of an active and creative group.

Correlation. Co-operation and correlation with other subjects can often be fruitful, especially in the creation, say, of stage sets for school plays. But it is essential that in correlating art with other subjects the creative aspects of art teaching are never lost sight of. Correlation should neither interfere with the unity of the art course as such, nor permit the unimaginative copying of book illustrations for project work in such subjects as history and geography.

Taste and appreciation. This phase of the work should always be closely related to the pupil's own experiences in two- and three-dimensional form. They should be encouraged to adopt a lively, sensitive and critical awareness of their surroundings. They should be given many opportunities to see a wealth of art masterpieces both of the present and the past, and of good examples of domestic and industrial design. In discussion the individual qualities of the work should be studied apart from its social setting and relation to other works of art.

Reference books on the theory and method of art education:

V. Loewenfeld, *The Nature of Creative Activity* (Kegan Paul, London, 1939).

V. Loewenfeld, *Creative and Mental Growth* (Macmillan, New York, 1952).

R. Mock, *Principles of Art Teaching* (University of London Press, London, 1955).

C. D. and M. R. Gaitskell, *Art Education during Adolescence* (Harcourt Brace, New York, 1954).

H. Read, *Education through Art* (Faber & Faber, London, 1943).

Education and Art (UNESCO, Paris, 1953).

Art Education. Ministry of Education Pamphlet, No. 6. Her Majesty's Stationery Office, London, 1946.

The Journal of the Art Teachers' Association of Victoria.

THE FIRST AND SECOND YEARS

Practice

Expression in colour. Pupils should be allowed many opportunities in class to paint lively, enjoyable and colourful subjects suited to the range of their interests and experience. In order to promote spontaneity and fluency in expression, large, long-handled bristle brushes, paper of at least half-imperial size (22 in. x 15 in.), and opaque paint such as powder and poster colour are essential. In the early stages of the course preliminary outline drawing is undesirable since it tends to lead to a timid, hesitant, 'neat' style.

Expression in line and wash. Having attained the capacity to fill large spaces with colour with some confidence pupils may be introduced to more graphic forms of expression. Many will, in these years, tend to rely increasingly upon their visual observations in creative work. Observations quickly rendered in line and wash will bring the pupil into touch with many of the problems of representational drawing. Subjects might vary from figures in action and at rest, running, leaping, dancing, resting, sleeping, etc. They might include landscapes, interiors, natural objects of the countryside, sea and shore, animals, trees, plants and flowers. Such subjects (and many more which will suggest themselves) might be drawn singly or in groups, from life or from memory.

Expression in three dimensions. Pupils should be given the oppor-

19 An art lesson in the school grounds, Firbank, Church of England
Girls' Grammar School, Sandringham, Victoria

20 Teacher trainees of the
sculpture class, 1958,
Kindergarten
Training College,
Madden Grove, Kew,
Melbourne
Lecturer:
Anita Aarons

21 A teacher trainee of the
painting class, 1958,
Kindergarten
Training College,
Madden Grove, Kew
Lecturer:
Frances Derham

Art is integrated with other
studies and with the student's
personal interests. She works
in many media at her own
adult level, and also studies
how similar media may be used
appropriately by children.

tunity for experimenting with both abstract and naturalistic forms in three dimensions. They might model and carve in such plastic forms as clay, soft stone, plaster, *papier maché,* soap, 'green' concrete, etc. They might construct freely in such *natural* materials as wool, feathers, leather, raffia, straw, reeds, bamboo, shells, bark, branches, acorns, pine cones, sand, small stones; and in such *artificial* materials as cotton wool, cotton, linen, silk, thread, string, card, woodshavings, linoleum, paper, glass, wire and metal, cotton reels, buttons, and milk bottle tops.

Lettering, pattern-making and abstract design. Rhythmic patterns introducing simple units in paint (e.g. finger painting, free brush and colour work, pastel and wet paper), cut-paper, block-printing (cork-, potato- and lino-cut, etc.). Non-repeating designs introducing asymmetrical and abstract patterns both free (such as scribble patterns) and rectilinear, involving the use of abstract shapes and colour. *Collages* of cut-paper, felt, fabrics, card of various textures, paint, etc. *Lettering* should be introduced as free lettering executed with chisel-ended and disc-ended nibs or by means of cut-paper lettering.

Taste and appreciation

Art appreciation. Pupils should be encouraged to discuss each other's work with the assistance of the teacher, searching always for those qualities which make different kinds of work interesting. Unfriendly and destructive criticism is to be avoided. A large variety of good works of art should be studied: *originals* where possible by visits to galleries, travelling exhibitions and private collections; *good quality colour prints* of modern and old masters; *lantern slides,* preferably coloured. Pupils should be shown many illustrations of masterpieces of architecture, sculpture and painting of all periods. In most cases it will be necessary to tell the pupils only a little about the artist and the times in which he lived: the aim being recognition, enjoyment, discussion and appreciation rather than the facts of history.

Taste in domestic and industrial design. The arrangement of classroom paintings on display, and the art room as a whole, its furniture, storage, illustrations, flowers, etc., might be discussed, and lead to the question of art in the home: kitchenware, curtains, carpets, furniture, etc. Classroom displays of well-designed and poorly-designed objects should be assembled. The purpose of these discussions will be to arouse a lively and discriminating taste, and will not always lead—

though it may at times—to the conclusion that the most recent mode is the best.

Architectural appreciation. Taste in architecture may be developed by discussing interesting buildings in the neighbourhood of the school which pupils should study for themselves or during excursions. New buildings, whether civic, commercial, ecclesiastic or domestic might be discussed together with any local ventures or problems in town planning.

Books recommended for use by first and second year pupils:

A. C. Ward, *Enjoying Paintings* (Penguin, 1954).

Biographies of Leonardo da Vinci, Michelangelo and Vincent van Gogh, by E. Ripley (O.U.P., New York).

THE THIRD YEAR

Practice

Expression in colour, line and mixed media. The fluency and breadth encouraged in the work of the first and second years should be preserved. But most pupils in the third year will desire to incorporate in their sketching from nature and the object an increased skill in recording observations, and will prefer themes suited to their widening interests and experiences in their inventive compositions. The teacher should encourage the pupil to acquire these skills where he has need of them. But skills should not be taught by rule of thumb methods (blackboard lessons in perspective, short-cut methods of figure drawing, colour theory, and the like). They may be taught by confronting individual pupils or groups of pupils with technical problems in a creative context: thus, figures in an interior will introduce both perspective and figure drawing. The stimulus provided by experimenting with a considerable variety of media is important. Pupils should be encouraged to experiment with different types of paper, choosing their own papers for the type of work in hand. They should experiment with a wide variety of graphic media: e.g. charcoal, lumber crayon, coloured pencils, wax, pastels, and with mixed media, such as charcoal and watercolour, calcimine scraper techniques, etc., etc. Quick, free line drawing in pencils and pens of various types will assist in developing skill in recording observations.

Expression in three dimensions. The plastic and constructive work of the first two years should be continued at a more advanced level.

The possibilities and limitations of the materials used will be discussed with a view to using them in ways appropriate to their true nature. The aesthetic and functional possibilities of using materials in varied combinations should be investigated. Design problems both of an *abstract* (such as the construction of tall, cubic, curved and horizontal structures), and of a *concrete* (such as a bridge, tunnel and shelter shed) nature might be attempted. In this work constructive principles, post and lintel, arch, dome, cantilever, suspension, and so on, will be discussed. Some mobile sculpture might be attempted. A wider range of hand-tools from those used in earlier years, and of various types, could be adopted; and the relation between tools and materials discussed. This section of the work should be continually correlated with training in taste and appreciation.

Lettering, pattern-making and abstract design. Pupils should experiment with basic types of lettering suited to various instruments, such as pen, brush, and paper-cut letters. Lettering should always be considered an integral part of the design problem in hand, and its style, size and situation should always be related to the purpose for which it is intended. When it is introduced into such activities as poster designing, book covering and the designing of notices, simple arrangements should be encouraged. Pattern-making and design may be developed along lines begun during the first two years of the course, using a wide variety of suitable materials. Pupils should experiment with line, shape, colour and texture, to produce simple and effective patterns. This work may be associated profitably with the study of good original examples of modern textile design.

Taste and appreciation

Art appreciation. While the emphasis should continue to be placed on the discussion of individual works of art, teachers should introduce, by means of the selection of a number of representative examples (in architecture, sculpture and painting), some awareness of the characteristic qualities of style of the main forms of art which have contributed to European culture: Egyptian, Greek, Roman, Byzantine, Romanesque, Gothic, Renaissance, Baroque, etc., together with some appreciation of Australian art, and of the Contemporary Movement. Some introduction to non-European art forms: Japanese, Chinese, Indian, Persian, Mexican, the Pacific, etc., may also be attempted where desired. It is neither expected that the teacher should necessarily cover all the periods mentioned nor that he should confine himself to those mentioned. In practice a very wide variety of works from various periods should be discussed from actual examples. Detailed book knowledge is not required. These discussions will provide a good basis for the survey course in the fourth year.

Architectural appreciation. Apart from the appreciation of buildings through the discussion of illustrations pupils should be encouraged to develop their interest in the architecture of their neighbourhood. They might, for example, assemble lists of buildings in the neighbourhood worthy of preservation, giving their reasons. Prominent errors of taste in local building design and civic planning could also receive attention. Some pupils will wish to compile photographic records, others to sketch plans and elevations of local buildings.

THE FOURTH YEAR

Work should be continued along lines suggested for the previous three years, provision being made at all times for the maturing interests and increasing skills of the pupils. Imaginative work should be interrelated with drawing from reality and other forms of art in which observation is called into play. Considerable breadth of experience in a variety of media is most desirable. Work should certainly not be limited to the minimum required by the Intermediate Examination. Whilst pupils will still need the stimulus of a variety of materials it is expected that many will select two or three media most to their liking, and seek to develop special creative abilities in them. Work in three dimensions should lead to a full awareness of the limitations and possibilities of materials. Where designing for a purpose is intended pupils should work out their design in terms of the material to be used. See also the details for the Intermediate Examination, below.

THE FIFTH YEAR

See details for the Leaving Examination, below.

THE SIXTH YEAR

See details for the Matriculation Examination, below.

DETAILS OF SUBJECTS
School Intermediate Examination
The examination will consist of two parts: (a) the practice of art.

(b) the appreciation of art. Part (a) will carry twice as many marks as Part (b).

(a) *The practice of art.* Candidates are required to submit six examples of original work executed during the year. The selection should present a variety of subject matter and be expressed in at least two varieties of media. The work is to be submitted in a *flat* container of uniform size (23 in. x 16 in.), made of strong paper. It should be possible for the examiners to remove and replace the work in the container without difficulty. Photographs of plastic and three-dimensional work can be included but are not required. The candidate's number is to be marked clearly at the top right hand corner of each sheet. *Do not fasten the sheets together.* The work is to be certified as the candidate's own original work of the current year by the Principal and the Art Teacher, and must reach the Registrar's Office, University, not later than the day of the written examination in Appreciation of Art.

(b) *The appreciation of art.* This will consist of a written paper of two hours' duration. It will cover the following sections which may be considered of equal value:

(i) An introduction to the Greek, Byzantine, Romanesque, Gothic and Renaissance periods of art.

Treatment should be confined to an examination and discussion of a few representative examples of the architecture, sculpture and painting of each of the periods mentioned. Pupils should be able to recognize and discuss the characteristic features of the styles in question, and be able to compare one with another. Detailed treatment of development and change within a single style is not required, nor detailed treatments of individual artists' works. Candidates, however, should have a general knowledge of the social, political and religious background of the periods dealt with in order to be able to discuss works of art in their social setting. This need only be brief *and should always be subordinated to the discussion of individual examples.* Every opportunity should be taken to study original examples in the National Gallery of Victoria.

(ii) European Painting since 1870: Impressionism, Post-Impressionism, and trends in art since 1900.

(iii) Australian art since 1880, with emphasis mainly upon the Heidelberg School and the Contemporary Movement.

(iv) An introductory study of present-day design in association with the home: domestic architecture, implements and appliances, furniture, fabrics, and ceramics. Pupils should, wherever possible, study actual examples.

Useful texts for teacher and pupil:

H. W. Janson and D. J. Janson, *The Story of Painting for Young People* (Abrams, 1952).

E. H. Gombrich, *The Story of Art* (Phaidon, London, 1955).

U. Hoff, J. Lindsay and A. McCulloch, *Masterpieces of Art in the National Gallery of Victoria* (Cheshire, Melbourne, 1949).

Architecture and Arts (periodical), Melbourne.

School Leaving Examination

The examination will consist of two parts: (a) the practice of art, (b) the appreciation of art. Part (a) will carry twice as many marks as Part (b).

(a) *The practice of art.* Candidates are required to submit six examples of original work executed during the year. The selection should present a variety of subject matter and be expressed in at least two varieties of media. The work is to be submitted in a *flat* container of uniform size (23 in. x 16 in), made of strong paper. It should be possible for the examiners to remove and replace the work in the container without difficulty. Photographs of plastic and three-dimensional work can be included but are not required. The candidate's number is to be marked clearly at the top right hand corner of each sheet. *Do not fasten the sheets together.* The work is to be certified as the candidate's own original work of the current year by the Principal and the Art Teacher, and must reach the Registrar's Office, University, not later than the day of the written examination in Appreciation of Art.

(b) *The appreciation of art.* This will consist of a written paper of two hours' duration which will be divided into two sections. Section (i) will carry twice as many marks as Section (ii).

(i) A study of Egyptian, Greek, Roman, Byzantine, Romanesque and Gothic art.

Treatment should proceed along lines suggested for the Intermediate Examination but with greater detail. Continuous study and discussion in class of a liberal variety of masterpieces chosen from the architecture, sculpture and painting of the periods mentioned are desirable, so that candidates may gain confidence in discussing the style, medium and social setting of masterpieces of art. The candidates should be given many opportunities for writing brief appreciative and critical accounts of works studied in class. Every opportunity should be taken to study original examples in the National Gallery of Victoria.

(ii) An introductory study of contemporary domestic and industrial design with special reference to modern processes and materials.

or

A study of twentieth century painting and sculpture.

Prescribed text:

E. H. Gombrich, *The Story of Art* (Phaidon, London, 1955). From ch. 1 to ch. 11 inclusive, and *for those including a study of contemporary painting in their course,* chs. 25, 26 and 27 also.

Additional Reading:

N. Pevsner, *An Outline of European Architecture* (Pelican, 1943).

U. Hoff, J. Lindsay and A. McCulloch, *Masterpieces of Art in the National Gallery of Victoria* (Cheshire, Melbourne, 1949).

A. Bertram, *Design* (Pelican, 1938).

Architecture and Arts (periodical), Melbourne.

The Matriculation Examination

The examination will consist of three parts: (a) work submitted, (b) an examination of three hours' duration in the appreciation of art, (c) an examination of three hours' duration in Painting and Drawing. Parts (a) and (c) will each carry half the number of marks of Part (b).

(a) *Work submitted.* Candidates are required to submit six examples of work executed during the year. The selection should show a variety of subject matter. The work is to be submitted in a *flat* container of uniform size (23 in. x 16 in.), made of strong paper. It should be possible for the examiners to remove and replace the work in the container without difficulty. Photographs of plastic and three-dimensional work can be included but are not required. The candidate's number is to be marked clearly at the top right hand corner of each sheet. *Do not fasten the sheets together.* The work is to be certified as the candidate's own original work of the current year by the Principal and the Art Teacher, and must reach the Registrar's Office,

University, not later than the day of the written examination in Appreciation of Art.

(b) *The appreciation of art*. The paper will cover the following three sections. It is expected that the time spent on section (ii) will be at least equal to the time spent on sections (i) and (iii) together.

(i) A survey of Egyptian, Greek, Roman, Byzantine, Romanesque and Gothic art.

This section will consist of a revision of work done in previous years. It will only be necessary for candidates to distinguish and discuss typical masterpieces of art of the periods mentioned.

(ii) A special study of Renaissance, Mannerist, and Baroque architecture, sculpture and painting. Consideration should be given particularly to the work of outstanding artists of each period.

(iii) A study of twentieth century architecture, with reference to materials, building processes, and the functions for which the architecture is intended.

(c) *Painting and drawing*. This will be a practical examination of three hours' duration at a centre specified. The paper will be divided into two sections. The first section will enumerate objects from which candidates may assemble a still-life. The second section will specify subjects from any of which a painting may be executed. Candidates may choose to work either in the first or second section. Only one drawing or painting will be required.

Prescribed text:
E. H. Gombrich, *The Story of Art* (Phaidon, London, 1955). Ch. 12 to ch. 22 (both inclusive).

Additional reading:
C. Gould, *An Introduction to Renaissance Painting* (Phaidon, London, 1957).
H. Woelfflin, *Classic Art* (Phaidon, London, 1953).
H. Woelfflin, *Principles of Art History* (New York, n.d.).
B. Berenson, *The Italian Painters of the Renaissance* (Phaidon, London, 1953).

(It is expected that teachers will make use of good special studies of individual artists and periods to supplement works of a general nature, e.g. the Phaidon Press publications.)

12

Art Education in New South Wales, Western Australia and Queensland

NEW SOUTH WALES

Nursery and Infant Schools. The child in the nursery school (the state controls four such schools) is given large pieces of newsprint paper and some dry colour or coloured starch with large brushes and encouraged to paint. The teacher asks the child about the picture to encourage oral expression and sometimes notes the answers near the symbols for reference later. The choice of subject is free and no instruction of any kind is given.

In infants' schools the child in first and second classes, but not in transition or kindergarten, draws some definite subject, with materials that are provided by parents' or mothers' clubs and this is followed by a talk about the pictures. Well-trained infants distribute their materials and display their pictures on lines with pins or clothes pegs. They tell each other about their pictures and say which they like best. They often say, for instance, that the figure is large or clear or bright or light or dark.

Popular subjects are themselves, their family, and things they are interested in. Apart from set subjects, such as 'Myself Combing My Hair', they have choice in such things as 'What I did in the Holidays'. Simple stripe patterns and movement patterns to nursery rhymes are attempted. Children stand up or sit down. Some schools have easels; they all use whatever materials they can get since art materials for infants are not supplied by the Department of Education.

Primary and Secondary Schools. In primary schools there is one hour per week devoted to art. This can be in two half-hour periods or one hour period. The subject is motivated briefly by the class teacher and a display and discussion follows all work. Where teachers have them, reference to pictures is made for purposes of comparison. The use of modern pictures is preferred, because they have greater freedom and colour.

75

There is no special room for art in the primary school, but some watercolours, brushes and paper, are provided. (£5,000 is available for art education in the whole state of 400,000 children.) Some lithographs have been provided to schools and schools may now buy further supplies of paints through government stores.

In primary schools some 70,000 children paint pictures from school broadcasts given once a fortnight.

In secondary education art is taught to all girls in home science schools, and to some of the girls, those taking one language, in high schools. Only a few schools have an art room for the purpose. In the metropolitan area, boys' high schools do not include art in the curriculum, but about six boys' secondary junior technical schools include art in the curriculum.

The number of forty-minute periods is from two to three in junior classes, but up to five for Leaving Certificate. Usually these are double periods. In the country districts some boys have the opportunity of taking art.

Art in secondary schools is taught by specialist teachers of whom there are sixty-four in the metropolitan area and forty-one in the country. Art is taken for the Intermediate and Leaving Certificate examinations. Many pupils who sit for Leaving Certificate art are rejects from other subjects who have been asked to take art as an alternative.

The Department of Education supplies equipment and materials to the value of £3,000 to secondary schools and £1,500 to opportunity centres.

Teacher-Training. For the Leaving Certificate candidates are examined by a committee who nominate them for art training at the East Sydney Technical College. This technical college is administered by the Department of Technical Education. The training here in drawing, design, painting, craft and sculpture takes three years. After one further year at Teachers' College, the teachers enter the department with a provisional certificate and graduate rates of pay. Lecturers in art are employed at all teachers' colleges.

Supervision. Art education in the state is supervised by one supervisor and one assistant. They are responsible for refresher courses, in-training, inspections, requisition and distribution of materials, demonstrations of method, Leaving Certificate examination and the syllabus.

WESTERN AUSTRALIA

Primary and Secondary Arts and Crafts. It is the policy of the Education Department to avoid specialization at the primary level. Art in the infants' and primary schools is conducted by the class teacher as a normal part of class activity. The curriculum for primary and secondary schools is at present being revised. But they will retain the same breadth and balance as the 1940 and 1948 syllabuses, and will provide for further integration with other subjects and a project-method approach. A course in crafts for primary schools was introduced in 1953. The value of crafts has an integrating quality and our future policy will be to use crafts as a means of vitalizing and enriching the whole life of the child both at school and elsewhere.

The secondary school art syllabus is at present being revised and a craft syllabus is in the planning stage. In all the five-year and three-year high schools and in most of the junior high schools art is carried on by art teachers who have been appointed through advertisement. Avenues of promotion through senior assistants to deputy heads are possible to these teachers. All art and craft materials are in short supply or simply impossible to obtain. Paint brushes, particularly watercolour sable type brushes, watercolour tubes or pastes, powder paints and oil colours are unprocurable. Papers suitable for use by infants or for fine watercolour work are difficult to obtain and are high in price. The teaching of art in Western Australia is considerably hampered by this lack of materials. Colour merchants are experiencing great difficulty in importing the materials required as a result of import licence restrictions. The teaching of art is also seriously handicapped by a shortage of furniture and buildings.

It is hoped that it will be possible to introduce a scheme which will make it possible, by the appointment of extra high school art teachers, to move senior art teachers in high schools to the neighbouring primary schools. Here they would act in an advisory capacity and provide a guide to art teaching preliminary to the high school course. This will also allow some experimental work to be carried out, and bring about a measure of decentralization.

Teacher-Training and the Teachers' Colleges. Two courses in arts and crafts are in operation: one, a basic course for the training of general practitioner teachers and the other an elective course for specialists. Lectures in the basic course cover educational and psychological principles; the importance of child art; theories of vision, colour, and perception; an introduction to the history of art; and classroom practice. The practical work is designed to give satisfaction to the student in the development of his own personality and his teaching ability. The specialists taking the elective course are expected to carry their theoretical studies to a higher level, to become acquainted with experimental work in the schools, and to explore a wide range of media in their practical work. Apart from these two main courses, secondary school, home science and manual teacher trainees are also catered for. An art club is very active, and sketching camps over the long week-ends are frequently arranged by the students themselves.

As a result of a bursary system in fourth- and fifth-year high schools, generous in-college allowances, and reasonably high teacher salaries, a record number of both artists and trainees are now being attracted into the profession. From this number specialists of a fairly high standard can be selected and prospects are bright for a continuous supply of art teachers for a number of years. The art teachers' course at the Perth Technical College provides training through Art Teachers' Certificates Parts I and II to the Art Teachers' Diploma. Examinations for the Art Teachers' Certificate and Diploma are jointly conducted by the Superintendent of Art and by the art master of the Perth Technical College.

In the teachers' colleges, although space and equipment are largely makeshift and inadequate, the greatest obstructions to full efficiency are the large numbers of students and the shortage of lecture time. A two-year basic course is really necessary, and for specialists a third or fourth year extension.

Supervision and Inspection. The Superintendent of Arts and Crafts is the responsible officer for the writing of reports on his subject in schools at all levels and on teachers solely occupied in the teaching of the subject. He is a member of the High School Inspectorial Panel and contributes to the school reports. A number of advisory teachers have been appointed to assist the Superintendent in the field. The conduct of schools of instruction for teachers, the arrangement and display of exhibitions, demonstrating, and advisory visits to schools and classes, etc. are among the duties of these specialists. The reaction of teachers to these visiting advisory teachers has been invariably most enthusiastic. Requests from schools for visits by these specialists come in constantly and there is always a back-lag. Under the super-vision of the Superintendent of Teacher-Training a continuous series of in-service courses are being conducted for headmasters and teachers. The Superintendent of Art and teachers' college lecturers in arts and crafts assist in conducting the classes. Schools of instruction in art and crafts both in city and country areas are conducted frequently by members of the art and crafts staff.

The Jubilee Art Committee of 1951 lodged the Jubilee Art Unit (a 20-cwt. van and a set of exhibition boards) in the keeping of the Education Department. This is available to any organization, including the art branch of the department, which is fostering art in Western Australia. Its services have made possible an almost continuous series of exhibitions in metropolitan and country areas. The most important of the exhibitions arranged by the art and crafts branch include the Annual Royal Show children's display, the travelling exhibitions spon-sored by UNESCO and the Commonwealth Office of Education, and the exhibitions arranged through the art gallery classes.

Art Gallery Classes. With the co-operation of the Director of the Art Gallery a programme of gallery classes was inaugurated in 1953. Second-year students from metropolitan high schools came to the gallery in groups of up to forty, and were introduced to the gallery, its functions, its collections, and some of the most important works of art. Only one visit per term was possible but they were so successful, and were received so enthusiastically by pupils, teachers and head-masters, that a much more ambitious programme is now attempted, and the service is being extended to older pupils of the high schools, to youth education groups and occasionally to adult groups. A full-time tours officer is to be appointed, and it will be his duty to make appropriate collections and arrange for their circulation.

Conclusion. Generally we have reason to be fairly satisfied about the position of art education in Western Australia. We are by no means smug but both our administrative organization and practice in the schools show promise of settling down into a satisfactory form. Our problems are many but they are clear-cut. With all possible assistance from the Department and sympathetic support from every-one concerned our task is relatively straightforward, and we hope ultimately to achieve something that will be looked on as a real contribution to education in our state.

QUEENSLAND

The Primary School. The aims of art education in Queensland as
set out in the 1952 Syllabus for Primary and Intermediate Schools
are threefold, namely: to give all children the opportunity to express
themselves creatively; to develop good taste and appreciation of the
best in the visual arts through specific activities performed under the
guidance and sympathetic encouragement of an understanding teacher;
and to develop co-ordination of muscular movements in the formation
of useful skills. Such skills may function later in some kind of
vocational training or in the pursuit of a useful hobby that will make
for better citizenship and the wise use of leisure.

The syllabus attempts to convey to the teacher the fundamental
idea that the only important standard for art is its originality. The
insistence on originality and 'learning through doing' is particularly
important during the manipulative, exploratory, and symbolic stages
of visual expression; that is, between the ages of four and seven years,
the teacher must not show the children 'how to draw' or allow
copying of any kind. They should be allowed to paint and draw,
model and construct, entirely from imagination and memory. In
picture-making and modelling activities the wise teacher makes full
use of the child's own interests and experiences as subject matter
for expression. Of course, it is the teacher's duty to provide the child
with fresh interests and experiences as he makes progress in other
subjects during his general course in education. These will supply
the need of further subject matter for free expression.

During the stage of transition, between the ages of eight and eleven
years, and corresponding to the period from Grade III to Grade V
in Queensland schools, a suitable balance is sought between creative
free expression and work directed by the teacher. Pictures and models
created by the children should express their own ideas, interests, and
daily experiences, and articles made in the handicraft lesson should
be useful and soundly constructed as well as being pleasing in shape,
colour and decoration.

After the age of eleven years it is realized that most children
approach the stage of realism. In Grades VI, VII and VIII it is found
that some children become discouraged with their efforts to express
original ideas and the tendency to copy from the work of others
becomes increasingly prevalent. As the child may lose interest because
he cannot produce results owing partly to his lack of technical know-

ledge and the need for constructive planning, the teacher is expected to give more attention to composition, proportion, detail and good finish than was necessary in lower grades.

The theories of colour and of perspective and foreshortening are explained only in so far as they act as an aid to expression. It is felt that over-dictation at this stage would be a mistake, but to avoid all dictation so that children will 'find out for themselves' would be equally wrong.

Drawing and painting from sight, as well as from imagination and memory, figure drawing from sight, elementary free perspective, experiments with various techniques and art media, colour knowledge, and practical design and construction are introduced gradually as the need arises when the child's work begins to falter because of an insufficient knowledge of technical principles.

The suggested time allotment for art and craft in primary schools is three hours per week, one hour of which is suggested for practical art and appreciating experiences, and two hours for handicraft. Teachers may make variations in this time allotment to suit local conditions.

In many of our schools the appreciation of art and nature is encouraged by surrounding the children with well chosen and colourful pictures inside the rooms and beautiful gardens outside. The Department has arranged for supplies of colour reproductions from the National Gallery of Victoria, which are supplied to schools on request.

All students attending the Queensland Teachers' College are given instruction in: practical art; handicraft (including paper and cardboard work and simple bookcrafts), and one craft selected from bookbinding, weaving, pottery and clay modelling, basketry, and leatherwork; the theory, history and appreciation of art; and the teaching of art and craft in schools. A total of three hours per week is devoted to art and craft. The methods of art and craft teaching in schools suggested to students are based entirely on the requirements of the syllabus for primary and intermediate schools. Four lecturers are employed full-time in the art and craft section of the college. To date, no course has been provided at the Teachers' College for those who wish to specialize as art teachers.

To implement the foregoing policy, both administrators and teachers are faced with many difficulties. Some of these difficulties are perhaps common to all states. We may list them as follows:

1. Enormous cost of supplying adequate equipment, tools, and

materials to all children, and insufficient government funds
voted to meet that cost.

2. Lack of space and workrooms to carry out many types of art
   and craft work that cannot be done in classrooms, also lack of
   storage space and cupboards for use in these rooms.

3. The introduction of methods of teaching art and craft to the
   large body of teachers in the schools who have not had the
   opportunity to attend refresher courses or to spend some time
   at in-service training. Handicraft is something new in Queensland schools and few teachers have received the necessary
   training to carry out the work efficiently.

4. The shortage of teachers which has led to over-large classes.
   It is most difficult for a teacher, even with training in the work,
   to carry out art and craft activities in overcrowded classrooms.

5. Misunderstanding of the aims of teaching art in schools by a
   large number of teachers and other persons, including parents
   and citizens generally.

6. The tendency by some to regard art and craft as an isolated
   subject in the curriculum and a luxury that can be dispensed
   with whenever extra time is needed for 'more important'
   examination subjects.

In Queensland, some grades in the infant school are supplied by
the Department with painting easels, brushes, powder paints, plasticine, crayons, paper, scissors and hand-work materials. Children in
other grades are supplied with small drawing books, erasers, and
lead pencils. All other art and craft equipment, tools, and materials
such as pastels, paints, brushes, knives, scissors, paper, clay, plasticine,
etc., have to be found from local school funds or purchased by the
parents.

At present, the success of art and craft work in many schools
depends largely on the enthusiasm and initiative of the teacher in
securing adequate supplies. It is realized that the responsibility of
finding materials places an undue burden on the teacher who has no
funds at his disposal other than what can be raised locally. Pastels
are too often used exclusively in our schools because they are cheap,
convenient, and expedient. Paints and brushes of reasonably good
quality are more expensive, but are absolutely necessary if real progress
is to be made in art education.

It is very difficult to get all teachers and parents to believe that

22 The Art Room, Preparatory School, Presbyterian Ladies' College, Burwood, Victoria

The Art Syllabus for Victorian Secondary Schools (1959) recommends: The room should be spacious and possess good light, and a supply of water. A smooth floor surface, preferably covered with linoleum, will greatly facilitate cleaning. Movable furniture is essential. Desks should be flat-topped to enable them to be moved together to make larger tables for group work. A number of adjustable easels should be provided. There should be ample cupboard space around the room, folio-racks, display boards, and, wherever possible, a store-room attached to the art room. Flat drawers will be needed for storing paper, bins for storing material used in three-dimensional work. It should be possible to darken the art room quickly for the purpose of showing slides. Every art room should be provided with its own projector — *See page* 64

23 An art class conducted by the Council of Adult Education, Victoria, at Pentridge Gaol. Tutor: Ian Bow

Art classes arranged at Pentridge Gaol have shown interesting results, but these classes are regarded as having a therapeutic and remedial aspect — Colin Badger, *page* 53 art has an important place in the development of the educated person. Children cannot be expected to develop good taste and appreciation if the teacher is completely indifferent to art and entirely lacking in taste. Far too many of our teachers still rely on antiquated stereotyped methods that are opposed to the spirit of the art and craft syllabus. The bad practice of copying 'scenes' and drawings of 'objects' from the blackboard has not been entirely eliminated in our schools. Many of the formal cut and paste exercises dictated to children, who blindly follow the teacher's instructions, produce uniform but uninspired results.

The Secondary School. The teaching of art in secondary schools has been confined mainly to preparing students for the Junior and Senior Public Examinations of the University of Queensland. The Junior paper is in two parts, viz.:

Part A: The Practice of Art

Part B: The Development and Theory of Art

The Practice of Art includes decorative design and colour application, freehand drawing and imaginative pictorial composition.

Part B, the Development and Theory of Art, includes some study of architecture and sections on European, British and Australian art. A knowledge of the principles of composition, an elementary knowledge of colour theory, the various mediums used and the meaning of various art terms is expected of the student during the two-year course.

The Senior paper is virtually an extension of the work for the Junior examination. Certain schools, such as the Domestic Science High School and the Industrial High School, provide classes without the examination stress; students have more liberty in the creative aspect of the subject.

Adult Education. Adult education in art covers the work of technical colleges, the Board of Adult Education and other means by which the Department of Education seeks to bring art before the people. Concerning technical schools, the art branch of the Central Technical College is the most important. It provides facilities for creative child art classes and its day and evening classes are open to students from adolescence onwards. A staff of twenty-four teachers is employed and the courses available follow the usual pattern of art schools, providing practical instruction in form, value and colour, with the application of design to the needs of industry. As is common to such schools, a percentage of students enter classes in order to equip themselves for more adequate art expression, and the Queensland Government gives encouragement by providing classes at a nominal fee.

Adult art classes are available at certain country colleges. The subjects taught are governed by local demand, which is mainly that of painting and commercial illustration. Craft work in the form of pottery-making, woodcarving, etc., is very popular. The Queensland Board of Adult Education carries art to districts which are not otherwise served by the Education Department's schools. Lecturers have been appointed to Brisbane, Ipswich, Kingaroy, Warwick, Maryborough, Nambour, Cairns, Atherton and Stanthorpe. From time to time, collections of original pictures and prints have been sent to the country, usually accompanied by a lecturer.

During 1951, the Queensland Government sponsored a special art train. This train, displaying paintings from the Queensland National Art Gallery, selected by Mr Robert Campbell, then Director of the Gallery, toured thousands of miles of Queensland's railway system, affording people in remote parts of the state an opportunity to view original works by Dobell, Murch, Gruner, Lambert, Phillips Fox, Rupert Bunny, Lloyd Rees, Hilder, Vida Lahey and others. The train, which carried a staff of four, was on tour for nine months.

The Aim of the Department of Education. Briefly, the aim of the Department is to foster among the people of its state an appreciation of art as a practical essential of everyday living. By training and importing art teachers who have a sound basic background, a broad tolerance of the individual's views and way of life, and whose interests keep them alive to contemporary developments, the Department hopes to keep abreast of current thought and trends in art education.

In accordance with the foregoing, it is the Department's policy to provide opportunity for all whose leaning is towards art to pursue, in the way best suited them, courses of study which would assist in developing to the full their latent talent. It is realized that art education involves more than the training of artists and the Department seeks with its available means to encourage the indigenous culture of the people as a whole.

Queensland is a large state with widely varying climatic conditions, and its population is fairly well decentralized. Diverse ways of life and sparseness of population introduce many difficulties. The Queenslander, by reason of climate, is essentially an out-of-doors person and the lack of long winter months when people are drawn together for study and exchange of ideas seems to account in some way for the generally superficial appreciation of the arts of other countries. However, post-war years have brought great changes and there is evidence of a general awakening to the importance of culture in the affairs of the people. Art is at its best when spontaneous, but one cannot deny the value of the fostering spirit afforded by those individuals and groups whose self-appointed task it is to see that art receives the recognition it deserves. The Department is keenly aware of the need for augmenting its art programme, but resources are not unlimited and the contribution to culture made by individuals, discussion groups, art bodies and others is noted and appreciated.

Appendix

The Melbourne UNESCO Art Seminar of 1954

RESOLUTIONS

For its working sessions the Melbourne Seminar divided itself into four groups which met separately, first for discussion, and then for the formulation of policy. Each group concerned itself with a particular field of art education, the four fields decided upon being: Art Education and the Child, Art and Secondary Schooling, Art in Adult Education, and Art and the Training of Teachers.[1] On the second last day of the conference these groups framed the results of their discussions into a series of resolutions, and on the final day these resolutions were submitted to the Seminar.

One of the striking features of the Seminar was the general agreement expressed by all members on the fundamental issues dealt with by the conference. On no issue did the Seminar find itself radically divided. The following resolutions were adopted:

INITIAL RESOLUTION

In order to identify itself with the Bristol Seminar the Melbourne Seminar adopted unanimously the following resolution based upon the conclusion arrived at in Bristol:

Art education should be based on creativeness; skill should develop in relation to the needs of expression. It is agreed that art education should develop taste. The purpose of art education is to assist the learner to grow intellectually, emotionally and socially.

GENERAL RESOLUTIONS

This Seminar of Australian art educationists

Believing that the neglect of the arts is a betrayal of an educational trust and can produce, if sufficiently general, an unimaginative, uncreative and emotionally sick community and

Believing that standards of taste are lower in Australia than most other countries,

[1] Names of the participants in each group are given on pp. 92-4.

86

Considers that standards must be raised and the environment made aesthetically stimulating through advice of experts in the various fields of art, architecture, cartography, domestic design, etc., and

Recommends that:

1. Governments and municipal and shire authorities should consult these experts as a matter of course.
2. The Australian Broadcasting Commission be urged to:
   (i) broadcast in the news sessions items of news of general interest relating to the arts;
   (ii) conduct regular sessions on art appreciation in a popular way over the national network as it does in connection with the other arts.
3. Consideration should be given to the establishment of a week devoted to good art and design.
4. The Commonwealth Government should be strongly urged to accept the responsibility for providing a continuous international exchange of exhibitions of the finest works of art obtainable.

ART EDUCATION AND THE SCHOOLS

(i)   General

This Seminar of Australian art educationists

Agreeing that art is a creative activity which enables the child to discover his own personality, and

Agreeing that art is a natural discipline whereby the child expresses emotion and communicates feeling in a social form, and

Agreeing that art is therefore a fundamental part of the educational process,

Considers that inspectors of schools and headmasters have a special duty to see that art is not neglected in the primary and secondary schools, and

Recommends that:

1. A seminar should be conducted for inspectors to assist them to become familiar with modern art education practice.
2. A number of artists should be included on committees which examine, advise on and report on:
   (i) all syllabuses,
   (ii) illustrative materials used in schools and the pictures dis-

played in schools with a view to removing those features which impede the creativity of children.

3. All art syllabuses should be revised every three years.
4. In each state there should be:
   (i) a superintendent of art with full inspectorial status;
   (ii) advisory teachers;
   (iii) the advice of professional artists and expert practitioners available to individual art teachers;
   (iv) access to the work of other schools in other states and countries.
5. All art *competitions* be discouraged since they are contrary to the principles of art education.

(ii) Primary Schools

This Seminar recommends that:

1. Art syllabuses should emphasize the creative aspect of art education and should present a challenge to the child's inventiveness.
2. Art education should develop the child's appreciation and understanding of the art and materials of the industrialized world in which we live by laying stress on experiments in construction with a variety of materials.

(iii) Secondary Schools

This Seminar recommends that:

1. Art should be accorded equal status in the schools with all other subjects.
2. The syllabus should provide a broad and balanced course of work in two and three dimensions (i.e. in drawing, painting, modelling and carving) set against a background of historical studies.
3. There should be sufficient amenities in the way of accommodation, furniture, equipment and materials, libraries and collections, projectors and teaching aids generally, to allow the teacher to conduct art work according to up-to-date methods.
4. These amenities should form a well designed environment and should conform to the teacher's own requirements and the teacher should, in addition, be free to give emphasis to his own

interests and abilities and to the local and domestic circumstances of his classes.

5. Art in secondary schools should be in the hands of specially trained art teachers.
6. The time allotted to art should be adequate for full participation by pupils and teachers and should include a minimum of one double period per week.
7. The practical sections of art should not be tested under examination room conditions but should be assessed by other means, such as a submission of certified work produced throughout the year.

(iv) Training of Teachers

This Seminar recommends that:

1. Teachers in the visual arts should enjoy the same standing as other teachers in the matter of prestige and in the matter of opportunity for promotion to the top positions in the service.
2. Visual arts subjects should be afforded the same status in higher education as academic or scientific subjects and teachers in the visual arts should enjoy the same opportunity as other teachers to obtain a university degree in their art subjects and to enter university courses in education.
3. (i) The courses of training for art teachers should give the art teacher specialized training and should entitle him to qualifications equal in value with those of other teachers with four years of training in arts, science, education, etc., and the standard of admission to this course of training should be equivalent to the standard of admission to courses of training in other fields of teaching.
   (ii) The course of training should be such that the teacher will have insight into both the aesthetic and the psychological characteristics of the work of children and such that he should be familiar with research methods.
4. Classes in teacher training should not contain more than twenty trainees and should allow a minimum of four periods per week for art and craft throughout the general course of training.
5. The study of art education and some experience in the visual arts should be an integral part of the training of all teachers and separate time should be allowed in such subjects as social

sciences, botany, nature study, etc., for training teachers in skills required to illustrate these subjects.

6. Teachers should be allowed sabbatical leave with a subsidy to undertake further study at home or abroad. Short periods for study leave should be available for approved reasons and in-service training should be available for senior personnel in the field of short intensive courses in art and art education.

7. The states should be requested to establish facilities for frequent interstate exchange of art teachers.

8. Educational authorities should establish the practice of sending art teachers abroad for further study and on exchange, and steps should be taken to see that art teachers' qualifications are recognized internationally.

9. To this end, a list should be made of those art diplomas and certificates of various authorities which may be granted parity and this list should be subject to periodical revision.

10. An Australian Association of Art Teachers should be formed and the individual state associations should affiliate with it, and it should affiliate with INSEA.[2]

ART AND ADULT EDUCATION

This Seminar recommends that:

1. Governments should be urged to provide adequate funds for the furtherance of the art education of adults.

2. Community participation in the visual arts should be encouraged by the various state authorities and by other means and the practice of holding summer schools, which includes the practice and appreciation of art, should be encouraged and extended throughout the community.

ART EDUCATION AND INSTITUTIONS OTHER THAN SCHOOLS

This Seminar recommends that:

1. Galleries and museums should be open seven days a week and at night.

2. Provision should be made for the exhibition of the work of living artists and designers and such exhibitions should be accessible to the public at all times.

[2] See p. 55.

3. Exhibitions should be organized of objects of art other than paintings and sculpture and such exhibitions should be widely circulated.

4. Every individual and organization connected with art education should continually draw the attention of the public to the fact that a reproduction can never take the place of an original work of art.

5. Provincial galleries and museums should be established in co-operation with local authorities and provided with advice and service from the national institutes.

6. Facilities should be provided in the Commonwealth of Australia for training professional staff for art galleries and museums.

7. In the vital matter of the constitution of state national gallery and museum boards, state government authorities should be urged to adopt the policy of limited (say, three-year) appointments to trusteeships. In making such appointments the state authorities should also clearly differentiate between the administrative functions of such appointees and the function of the gallery director who should be fully recognized as an art expert and be invested with complete autonomous power in the recommendation and purchase of works of art. It is highly desirable that, in the interest of public art collections and art education in general that the special abilities of businessmen and other persons for general business and diplomatic work in art galleries should be recognized and not confused with the functions of the director whose judgment in his own field is the result of a lifetime of experience.

INDIGENOUS ART

This Seminar, being strongly of the opinion that Western (or European) influence on aboriginal art constitutes a grave danger to that art and considering that there is an urgent need for preventive measures, recommends that a constructive and sympathetic policy be established and implemented to encourage and preserve the indigenous art of the natives of Australia and her external territories.

VISUAL ARTS IN THE UNIVERSITIES

This Seminar recommends that all Australian universities should be urged to establish chairs of Fine Arts.

PARTICIPANTS

Director of the Seminar:

Mr Bernard Smith, Lecturer in Fine Arts, University of Melbourne.

Executive Sub-Committee:

Mr D. Orban, Chairman, UNESCO Committee for the Visual Arts.

Mr J. Lipscomb, Representative of the Contemporary Art Society of Australia on the UNESCO Committee for the Visual Arts.

Mr T. S. Raggatt, Chairman, UNESCO Committee for Education.

Mr Bernard Smith.

Secretary:

Mr H. J. Russell, Senior Education Officer, International Relations, Commonwealth Office of Education.

Assistant Secretary:

Mr J. Ross, Commonwealth Office of Education.

Mrs G. Abbott, Representative of the Headmistresses' Association of Australia, New South Wales.

Mr C. R. Badger, Director, Council of Adult Education, Victoria.

Miss E. V. Bauld, Senior Art Teacher, Department of Education, Tasmania.

Mr I. Bow, Art Teacher, Haileybury College, Victoria.

Mr J. Bowen, Art Teacher, Department of Education, New South Wales.

Miss M. J. Braine, Art Lecturer, Claremont Teachers' College, Western Australia.

Mr H. R. Brown, Head of Applied Art Department and Vice-Principal, Royal Melbourne Technical College, Victoria.

Professor G. S. Browne, Professor of Education, University of Melbourne.

Dr W. Bryden, Director, Tasmanian Museum and Art Gallery, Hobart.

Professor J. T. Burke, Professor of Fine Arts, University of Melbourne.

Mr J. A. Campbell, Art Supervisor, Department of Education, Western Australia.

Mrs S. G. Coalstad, Council of Adult Education, Victoria.

Dr K. S. Cunningham, Director, Australian Council for Educational Research.

Mr J. Dabron, Art Supervisor, Department of Education, New South Wales.

Mr W. A. Dargie, representing the Royal Art Society of New South Wales.

Mr L. R. Davies, Acting Head of the Art School, East Sydney Technical College.

Mrs A. P. Derham, Victorian Kindergarten Training College and Associated Teachers' Institute, Melbourne.

Mr M. C. Dimmack, Lecturer in Art, Burwood Teachers' College, Victoria.

Mr G. Docking, Education Officer, National Gallery of Victoria.

Mrs S. Duldig, Art Teacher, St. Catherine's School, Victoria.

Mr N. R. Edwards, Chief Executive Officer, State Film Centre, Victoria.

Mr Peter Foldes, English artist and film producer, then visiting Australia.

Mr C. G. Gibbs, Art Teacher, Department of Education, Queensland.

Miss M. Grierson, Representative, New Educational Fellowship.

Mr V. Greenhalgh, Deputy Head of the Applied Art Department, Royal Melbourne Technical College.

Mrs J. Hammet, Psychiatric Social Worker, Royal Park Mental Hospital, Victoria.

Mr A. R. Henderson, formerly Deputy Chairman of Trustees, National Gallery of Victoria.

Dr L. Hirschfeld Mack, Art Master, Geelong Church of England Grammar School, Corio, Victoria.

Dr Ursula Hoff, Keeper of the Prints, National Gallery of Victoria.

Mr J. Hunt, Art Teacher, Department of Education, Western Australia.

Mr D. I. Johnston, Superintendent of Art, Department of Education, Victoria.

Mr Daryl Lindsay, Director, National Gallery of Victoria.

Miss L. Luly, Art Teacher, Presbyterian Ladies' College, Melbourne.

Mr F. D. McCarthy, Curator of Anthropology, Australian Museum, Sydney.

Mrs M. Macartney, Art Teacher, Lauriston School, Victoria.

Mr A. McCulloch, Art Critic, the *Herald*, Melbourne.

Mr F. C. Mellow, Senior Lecturer in Art, Teachers' College, Melbourne.

Mr J. W. Mills, Inspector of Secondary Schools, Department of Education, Victoria.

Mr Hal Missingham, Director, National Gallery of New South Wales.

Mr C. J. Nevill, Art Teacher, Department of Education, Western Australia.

Professor O. A. Oeser, Professor of Psychology, University of Melbourne.

Mr F. A. Philipp, Senior Lecturer, Department of Fine Arts, University of Melbourne.

Miss M. Rentoul, Art Teacher, Melbourne Church of England Girls' Grammar School.

Mrs L. H. Sherrard, President, New Education Fellowship.

Mr R. A. Simpson, Art Master, Camberwell Grammar School, Victoria.

Mrs H. Stevens, Council of Adult Education, Victoria.

Professor A. K. Stout, Professor of Moral and Political Philosophy, University of Sydney.

Father G. J. Sullivan, Catholic Education Department, Victoria.

Mr G. Thomson, Assistant Director, National Gallery of Victoria.

Mr T. F. Wilson, Representative on the UNESCO Committee for the Visual Arts of the Australian Commercial and Industrial Artists' Association.

WORKING GROUPS

Art Education and the Child

Mr T. S. Raggatt, *Convenor*	Mr J. Dabron
Mr C. J. Nevill, *Rapporteur*	Mrs L. H. Sherrard
Dr L. Hirschfeld Mack	Miss M. Grierson
Father G. J. Sullivan	

Art and Secondary Schooling

Mr J. A. Campbell, *Convenor*	Mr P. Foldes
Mrs G. Abbott, *Rapporteur*	Mr J. Lipscomb
Dr K. S. Cunningham	Miss E. V. Bauld
Mr H. R. Brown	Mrs M. Macartney
Mr J. W. Mills	Mr F. Philipp
Mrs S. Duldig	Miss L. Luly

Art in Adult Education

Mr A. R. Henderson, *Convenor*
Mr G. Docking, *Rapporteur*
Mrs S. G. Coalstad, *Rapporteur*
Mr D. Orban
Mr T. F. Wilson
Mr F. D. McCarthy

Mr L. R. Davies
Mrs J. Hammet
Dr W. Bryden
Mr I. Bow
Mr J. Hunt

Art and the Training of Teachers

Mr G. Thomson, *Convenor*
Mrs A. P. Derham, *Rapporteur*
Mr F. C. Mellow, *Rapporteur*
Miss M. J. Braine
Miss M. Rentoul
Mr M. C. Dimmack

Mr C. G. Gibbs
Mr V. Greenhalgh
Mr D. I. Johnston
Mr A. McCulloch
Mr H. Missingham

Index